"What an encouragement strategies that will help our anxious kids anchor in who God made them to be. Parents will find not only insights but also practical helps to apply to your situation. This is a resource I highly recommend."

Gregory L. Jantz, PhD, founder of The Center: A Place of HOPE; author of forty books

"*When Anxiety Roars* knocks it out of the park! For parents as well as professionals, this book provides a conceptual framework as well as practical, hands-on information and tools to assist children in maneuvering the landmines of anxiety. The emphasis of looking at the child separate from their anxiety is a wonderful reframe to help the child as well as the adult 'tame the lion.' This is one of the best resources on children and anxiety available on the market today!"

Lyn Grooters, LISW, therapist; prior social worker for thirty years, Des Moines Public Schools

"Holthaus is able to provide valuable guidance to parents regarding anxiety and emotions by explaining neurobiology that occurs at various developmental levels, and she connects with parents through applicable antidotes, scenarios, and explanations that are easy to understand through a biblical worldview. The education and coping skills she provides to parents who have a child struggling with anxiety are spot-on!"

Jana Vink, LISW, RPT-S, owner/clinician, Grace Counseling

"An easy-to-ready, very practical guide to help parents and loved ones know how to best identify the many facets of anxiety and how to best support children who are struggling. I appreciated this book's concrete conversations and activities, and I only wish I could have read this ten years ago, when we had four children in our home—but it's never too late! I highly recommend this to both parents and educators."

Jil Nelson, elementary school principal; mom of four young adults

"With great clarity and care, *When Anxiety Roars* guides parents into a deeper understanding of the very real anxiety and worry our children hold. This book is a wealth of knowledge—a well-researched resource spanning ages and stages, helping us better understand how God has wired our children's brains and bodies so that we might love them more fully. I'm sure to return to this book in the moments when I need the well-worn wisdom of another to help me walk with my children through the darkness, pointing them toward the One who never leaves nor forsakes us."

Kayla Craig, author of *To Light Their Way: A Collection of Prayers & Liturgies for Parents*

"*When Anxiety Roars* is a must-read for parents who see their child struggle with anxious thoughts and feelings. Holthaus helps parents deeply understand the nature of anxiety in children and provides meaningful instruction. Her approach empowers both the child and the parent."

Tamara Rosier, PhD, author of *Your Brain's Not Broken*

When Anxiety Roars

Partnering with Your Child
to Tame Worry and Anxiety

Jean Holthaus,
LISW, LMSW

Revell

a division of Baker Publishing Group
Grand Rapids, Michigan

Published by Revell
a division of Baker Publishing Group
PO Box 6287, Grand Rapids, MI 49516-6287
www.revellbooks.com

Printed in the United States of America

Library of Congress Cataloging-in-Publication Data
Names: Holthaus, Jean, 1963– author.
Title: When anxiety roars : partnering with your child to tame worry and anxiety / Jean Holthaus, LISW, LMSW.
Description: Grand Rapids, MI : Revell, a division of Baker Publishing Group, [2022]
Identifiers: LCCN 2021035600 | ISBN 9780800736088 (paperback) | ISBN 9780800741440 (casebound) | ISBN 9781493434251 (ebook)
Subjects: LCSH: Parenting—Religious aspects—Christianity. | Child rearing—Religious aspects—Christianity. | Parent and child—Religious aspects—Christianity. | Worry in children. | Anxiety in children. | Worry—Religious aspects—Christianity. | Anxiety—Religious aspects—Christianity.
Classification: LCC BV4529.H633 2022 | DDC 248.8/45—dc23
LC record available at https://lccn.loc.gov/2021035600

Unless otherwise indicated, Scripture quotations are from THE HOLY BIBLE, NEW INTERNATIONAL VERSION®, NIV® Copyright © 1973, 1978, 1984, 2011 by Biblica, Inc.® Used by permission. All rights reserved worldwide.

Scripture quotations labeled AMPC are from the Amplified® Bible (AMPC), copyright © 1954, 1958, 1962, 1964, 1965, 1987 by The Lockman Foundation. Used by permission. www.Lockman.org

Scripture quotations labeled GW are from GOD'S WORD®. © 1995, 2003, 2013, 2014, 2019, 2020 by God's Word to the Nations Mission Society. Used by permission.

Scripture quotations labeled ICB are from the International Children's Bible®, copyright ©1986, 1988, 1999, 2015 by Tommy Nelson. Used by permission.

Scripture quotations labeled KJV are from the King James Version of the Bible.

Scripture quotations labeled TLB are from The Living Bible, copyright © 1971. Used by permission of Tyndale House Publishers, Inc., Carol Stream, Illinois 60188. All rights reserved.

22 23 24 25 26 27 28   7 6 5 4 3 2 1

Contents

This book is dedicated to all those endeavoring to
"Start children off on the way they should go." (Prov. 22:6).
I pray the content of this book can affirm and assist you
as you invest into the lives of children.

Acknowledgments

While this book contains one author's name, it is actually a compilation created by many authors who have traversed through deserts, scaled mountains, and carefully picked their way through the deepest of valleys alongside me on my journey as both a parent and a therapist. I can't identify and name each author, but all are important and I am grateful for the sacrifice, love, and investment each has made.

First and foremost, I am grateful for Jesus, who relentlessly and passionately pursued me from the moment I drew my first breath. His persistent love has changed my life and enabled me to risk venturing into the unknown and exploring who he created me to be instead of staying within the safety of what I could readily envision. I can't imagine life without my kinsman redeemer, bridegroom, and friend.

Michelle and Michael, you patiently and graciously taught me how to be a parent and how to parent you. Your willingness to forgive and trust again when I failed you is a precious gift that I treasure. Michelle, you are a woman of deep compassion whose desire to care for and serve others uniquely reflects the heart of Jesus. I experience profound joy as I watch you chose to live life fully and refuse to shrink back into the illusion of safety within the shadows. Michael, your deep reservoir of strength intermingles with a kind and caring heart to create a beautiful mosaic. I am both awestruck and challenged by the ways you have navigated the valleys of your life and believe you will scale to heights you cannot possibly dream of.

Michael and Jeanne Hirsch, you coparent with me in many ways, and I am so grateful for your presence in my life and in the lives of my children. Thank you for the countless hours spent sharing life, sacrificially giving of yourselves, and just having fun together.

Suzanne Vogel, I am eternally grateful God brought you into my life and grateful for all the ways we have "mothered" together. You have relentlessly challenged me, boldly spoken truth to me, and passionately encouraged me as we have journeyed together. I look forward with anticipation to continuing the journey.

Don and Mary Orange, you lovingly opened your home and extended the precious gift of sharing life together. Our children spent many of their formative years together, and I learned so much about parenting from the two of you. Even though we now live states apart, I see the fruit of our time together in my life and in the lives of my children.

Cindy Peterson, Kathy Utterback, and Rita Schacherer, you have each been mentors and teachers along the way who have taken risks and invested in me personally and professionally. You modeled what it means to be a therapist who works with children. Thank you for all the ways you demonstrated so beautifully what being a therapist is truly about.

Andrea Doering, Lindsey Spoolstra, Erin Bartels, Olivia Peitsch, Sarah Traill, Eileen Hanson, Laura Klynstra, and everyone else at Baker Books involved in shepherding this book from conception to publication—you are amazing, and this book wouldn't exist without you! I am indebted to each of you for seeing potential, tirelessly editing, creating the cover design, and molding this book into something truly able to help those who read it.

Meghan Hirsch, I am grateful for the hours you spent turning my cryptic annotations into appropriate documentation, correcting formatting errors, and pointing out sentences that made no sense. Your time has been invaluable!

Finally, I give my thanks to the parents and children who have sat in my office over the last twenty-seven years. You have been the teachers through whom I have learned what it is like to struggle with anxiety or be the parent of an anxious child. The time I spent walking with and learning from you formed me as a therapist. Thank you for allowing me to share in your journey and learn from you. Without each of you, this book would not be possible.

ONE

Why Children Don't Act
and React like Adults

On April 23, at 1:20 a.m., Dr. Jackson laid a 7 lb. 10 oz. bundle in my arms. In that moment, I stepped into an unknown world nothing in life had truly prepared me for. I became the mother of an amazing little girl—and realized I had absolutely no idea what I was doing. I had a degree in elementary education and had taught students from kindergarten through eighth grade, but all that education and experience hadn't prepared me for the overwhelming sense of responsibility and inadequacy that accompanied this moment. Two days later, when my husband and I arrived home with our precious little girl, I walked into the living room, sat down, looked at her, and tearfully announced, "I don't know how to do this without the nurses." While I have no doubt part of this was the hormones, it remained a nagging feeling I experienced at various times throughout my years of childrearing.

I frequently wish parenting worked like baking. If you pick a good recipe and follow it exactly, you produce a wonderful dish every time. Unfortunately, there is no magic recipe for raising a child free from mental health concerns. You may resonate with my experience and be reading in hopes of finding answers to your questions and fears.

If you're constantly attempting to "do it right," I encourage you to let go of this ideal. There is only one perfect parent—our heavenly Father—and even his perfect parenting didn't produce perfect children! *All* his children, with the exception of Jesus, face ongoing struggles throughout their lives. Although this reality is found throughout Scripture, many of us—especially those raised in the church—grew up believing something different. We were either directly taught or concluded through conjecture that trusting in Christ as Lord and Savior, routinely doing what Scripture commands, and avoiding things Scripture admonishes against produces lives free of struggle and children who mature to be well-adjusted, competent, God-fearing adults. While this may sometimes be true, the Bible is replete with examples of those whose deep faith and devotion didn't prevent personal struggles, such as Paul's thorn in the flesh (1 Cor. 12:7), or whose children were far from problem-free, such as David's son and Eli's sons (2 Sam. 15–19; 1 Sam. 2:12).

All of us—parents and children alike—are journeying to become all we were created to be. I am much wiser and parent more effectively now than I did during my children's formative years. I once told my adult son I wished I could have a "do over" and parent his first eighteen years again with the knowledge and skill I now have. His response was to quip, "Mom, you would just make different mistakes." Alas, he spoke truth! Mercifully, God is forgiving, children are incredibly resilient, and perfect parenting isn't required to produce healthy adults. Our ability to parent effectively only grows when we approach parenting as a skill to be learned rather than something we should just know how to do.

You can incorporate the principles in this book into your parenting to foster your child's mental health and self-esteem and create an environment where they feel safe, well-loved, and competent. As you read, there will be places you are invited to explore your current parenting technique to determine what changes might help your child learn effective ways of coping with anxiety. This book will offer you new ways to think about and interact with your child, which, when mixed with what you already know of good parenting, will help you effectively parent your child when they are anxious *and* when they are joyously celebrating their most recent accomplishment.

To start this journey, we will explore some basic differences between toddlers, children, teens, and adults. This will help you understand how the children in your life function differently than you do, and it will also provide a common framework to utilize throughout the rest of the book.

Children's Brains

An infant is born with all the physiological structures of an adult in miniature form—including all the brain structures and all the neurons they will ever need. However, while infants and children physically resemble adults, anyone who has attempted to convince a screaming child there really isn't a monster under the bed can attest to the fact they don't think like adults. The human brain isn't fully mature until the midtwenties and continually changes throughout life.

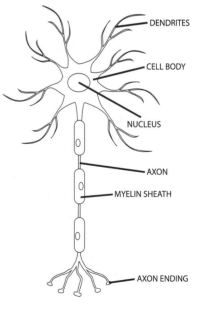

Neurons are the basic cells that make up the brain and the nervous system. Neurons receive input from the external world through the senses, transform the input into electrical signals, and relay those signals back and forth. This interaction of neurons forms our personality and our responses to the world around us.

15

Neurons are composed of a cell body, axons, and dendrites. Neurons produce energy in the form of various chemicals called *neurotransmitters*, which allow neurons to communicate with one another. Neurotransmitters flow down through the *axon* of one neuron into what is called the *synaptic cleft*—the gap between two neurons. They then attach to the receiving side, or *dendrite*, of a second neuron. This process is called a *synapse*.

As energy flows between neurons (firing) in the same pattern repeatedly, *neural pathways* are formed, causing specific thoughts, emotions, movements, and behavior patterns. While all neurons

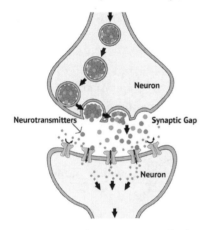

are present at birth, they haven't learned who to communicate with and in what order they need to communicate to create things like speech or controlled movement. This learning occurs over the course of our lifetime. However, during the first three years of life, a child's brain is growing faster than any other body part and forms over one thousand trillion connections between neurons.

At the same time, the brain is also engaged in a process called *myelination*, covering and insulating the axons of each neuron with layers of fat. When axons have been covered by this fat, called a *myelin sheath*, neurotransmitters can move along the neuron faster, which speeds up thinking and movement.

As neurons learn to fire together in sequence, the neurons used become stronger and faster. The brain simultaneously eliminates unused synapses and helps optimize the brain's functioning. This process of forming new neural pathways, called *neural plasticity*, continues throughout our lifetime as we learn and grow. The development of these neural pathways is heavily influenced by our experiences in life and our genetic code.

Your child's thoughts and ability to regulate their emotions differ from yours because different areas of the brain develop neural pathways at different rates. For example, the brain's *prefrontal cortex*, where reasoning and thinking through the consequences of decisions occurs, develops more slowly and doesn't fully mature until the midtwenties. In the rest of the chapter, we will explore the major differences in how children communicate, learn, and deal with emotions at different stages of development. You can read all the remaining sections of this chapter if the information seems helpful, but it may be better to skip to the section describing the stage of development your child is currently in, then consider reading the section before and after. As you read each of these three sections, pick out things that fit your child. Development doesn't occur at the same rate for all children, so you may find your child functioning above their chronological age in some categories and below it in others. The age breaks are generalizations and shouldn't be used to assess whether your child is ahead or behind where they "should" be. Next, read the last section in this chapter, "Applying What You Learned," to think about how to utilize what you have learned.

Birth to Two Years

Infants are born without the ability to voluntarily control their emotions or behavior. They don't have a sense of themselves as separate from their mothers until around age one. Infants and toddlers depend upon others to help them manage their emotions and to care for their needs. This does not, however, mean they don't communicate effectively.

Communication

Infants are born with the capacity to intuitively sense the emotions of people around them, to respond to the emotions of others, and to communicate what they are feeling to others. Eight-month-old Suzie wakes from her morning nap alone in her crib with an empty stomach. In her discomfort, she begins to whimper. When this does not summon her caregiver, her whimpers turn into cries and then wails. Her mother, listening to the baby monitor in the kitchen while attempting to finish washing dishes, feels mildly anxious when Suzie stirs and begins whimpering. As Suzie's cries intensify, so does her mother's anxiety. The bond between Suzie and her mother, combined with the anxiety and discomfort Suzie's crying creates within her mother, prompts Suzie's mother to stop washing dishes and begin warming a bottle. As Suzie's cries escalate to wails, her mother's anxiety also escalates and increases her longing to satisfy Suzie's needs so she will stop crying. She scoops Suzie up into her arms, gently rocking her while calmly talking to her and offering her a bottle. Mom's anxiety calms as she begins actively working to calm her child. Suzie senses her mother's calmness and this, combined with the bottle, soothes her fear so she relaxes into her mother's arms and receives the love and food she needs.

This ability to communicate, combined with the bond between parent and child, creates a symbiotic relationship in which parents are attuned to their child and attend to the child's needs, resulting in their child responding positively to having their emotional

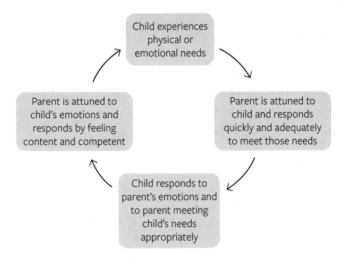

and physical needs met. This, in turn, causes parents to feel relaxed, content, and adequate. However, if something within this cycle breaks down, either the child's needs won't be met consistently or the parents' ability to feel content and competent will be threatened.

Learning and Memory

Infants and toddlers use their senses and motor skills to explore and understand their world. Developmental psychologists describe them as "little scientists" because they focus on doing things and seeing what happens as a result.[1] While adults have no conscious memory of the first years of life, they do remember the things learned during these years. Many of our memories from these first years are stored as visceral feelings without language to accompany them, making them difficult to recall as conscious memories.[2] For example, as a toddler my son was scared by a black dog much larger than he was. For years afterward, he would have a visible visceral reaction to large dogs (especially if they were black). He couldn't explain why he was afraid, but he was. His brain had stored the memory and was using it even though he couldn't recall it.

Emotions

Infants enter the world experiencing two primary groups of emotions: distress/pain and contentment/pleasure. Their emotional experiences expand over the first two years of life to include a wide array of instinctual and learned emotions.[3] Across cultures, infants express joy and laughter between two and four months,[4] anger is evident by six months,[5] and fear is easily identifiable by nine months.[6]

As infants and toddlers experiment, they learn what things to fear, both from their personal experiences and from the reactions of people around them. Dad's fearful reaction when Jonathan approaches the top of a flight of stairs without a gate teaches Jonathan stairs are dangerous. If he approaches stairs and tumbles down them, he learns through personal experience that stairs cause pain. Depending upon the child's temperament, they may need more personal experiences to learn or may easily become fearful based solely upon the fear and anxiety they perceive within the adults around them.

As a toddler's brain develops, they experience a wide range of intense emotions. They do not, however, possess the skills to articulate what they are feeling or to manage their feelings. They are dependent upon others to recognize their emotions and help manage them.

Early Childhood (Two to Six)

By the time a child is two, their brain already weighs 75 percent of what it will in adulthood, and when they are six, it weighs 90 percent of what it will in adulthood.[7] This does not, however, mean a six-year-old thinks almost the same way adults do. While all the structures are present, they are not "wired up" and able to respond like an adult. The brain continues to develop neural pathways and is especially focused on myelination during early childhood.[8] Myelination speeds thought processing, allowing the two-year-old who has to think about the name for an object to readily identify this same object without much thought at all by the time they're six.

Neurons have two kinds of impulses, *activating* and *inhibiting*. Adult brains know when to activate, so the individual acts on an impulse, and when to inhibit, so the individual resists the urge to act. However, this isn't something younger children can do. The poor impulse control that causes young children to flit between activities, touch things they've been told not to, and squirm around instead of sitting still is appropriate and normal. Their brains can also perseverate (get stuck) on one thing and have difficulty shifting away from it.[9] This is especially evident when attempting to get your five-year-old to stop playing and get ready for bed or to stop crying when they don't get their way. What appears to be defiance may be the brain getting stuck on something and having difficulty knowing how to shift gears to let go of this thought.

Communication

Two-year-olds have a vocabulary of between one hundred and two thousand words they use to create two- to six-word sentences. By the time they're six, their vocabulary has expanded to between three thousand and ten thousand words, and they form more intricate, complex sentences.[10] They use language to communicate about their internal world, ask questions (sometimes at the most inappropriate times) about their external world, and they learn the social rules for communicating effectively through trial and error. Three-year-old Zoe will frequently interrupt whoever is speaking when an exciting thought enters her mind, but by age six she can routinely restrain herself, wait her turn, and ask socially appropriate questions.

Learning and Memory

Cognitive theorist Jean Piaget uses the term *preoperational intelligence* to describe this stage of development. Preoperative children don't use logical reasoning processes but can represent objects with words.[11] Preoperational children understand the word *dog* represents the puppy they play with and know this puppy is alive. However, their thought processes are not logical, so they may believe a shirt or the wind is also alive. Their thought processes are also *egocentric*—centered around themselves. While this seems like selfishness, it isn't. They view everything from their perspective and don't have the ability to step outside of this to think about things from another's perspective. When my daughter was this age, she bought me Disney movies as Christmas presents, not out of selfishness but because she loved them so much she was sure I would also love them.

Preoperational thought causes children to see things as static and irreversible. A parent is a parent, and it isn't possible for them to have ever been a child. In the same way, if Danny requests a hamburger without pickles, and Dad mistakenly puts pickles on it, taking the pickles off doesn't change the hamburger into one without pickles. Once the hamburger has pickles on it, it becomes a hamburger with pickles in Danny's mind (even after he sees Dad remove the pickles). This isn't changeable, so Danny will likely refuse to eat the hamburger.

Children work to understand their world and, as part of this, develop theories to explain things they don't understand.[12] Combining this with a child's egocentric view causes them to operate from theories like "everyone intends to do things correctly." A child operating from this theory will watch a cartoon where one character is willing to ride a bike and the other isn't and conclude one character knows their bike is unsafe while the other character knows their bike is safe. In this same way, they have difficulty believing parents would ever intend to do anything other than what is correct and don't understand why parents would ever think the child did something wrong on purpose.

Emotions

Emotion regulation skills begin developing in early childhood and continue growing throughout life.[13] These skills are learned by observation and imitation and through direct teaching. The *limbic system* is crucial in the development of emotion regulation skills.

The *amygdala* is the structure within the brain that registers both positive and negative emotions. It is the place where fear first registers.[14] As activity within this brain region increases during early childhood, so does the prevalence of overwhelming terror. This, in turn, results in incidents like Carla crying hysterically when asked to ride an escalator with her parents. When this happens, parents often attempt to reason with their child and become

Limbic System

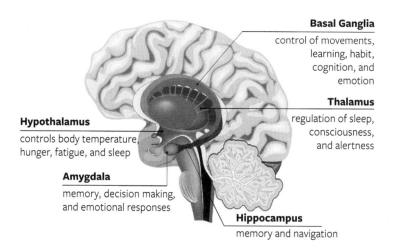

Basal Ganglia
control of movements, learning, habit, cognition, and emotion

Thalamus
regulation of sleep, consciousness, and alertness

Hypothalamus
controls body temperature, hunger, fatigue, and sleep

Amygdala
memory, decision making, and emotional responses

Hippocampus
memory and navigation

frustrated when the child doesn't calm in response. However, the amygdala isn't logical. It responds to comforting, not logic.

The second structure within the limbic system that affects emotion regulation is the *hippocampus*. When the amygdala reacts with fear over being asked to ride the escalator, the hippocampus, which processes memory, kicks in to help recall memories of similar experiences. If Carla remembers a previous fun escalator ride, she may begin to calm. Conversely, if the hippocampus supplies a similar scary situation from the past, it will intensify Carla's fear.[15] Both the amygdala's fear and the hippocampus's response happen instinctually, without any conscious thought on Carla's part.

The amygdala sounds the alarm, and the hippocampus either dampens or intensifies this alarm. The *hypothalamus* responds to the signals from both structures by producing cortisol, oxytocin, and other hormones to activate the appropriate brain and body structures. Ideally, the hypothalamus reacts in moderation and produces just the right amount of chemicals to appropriately respond to the situation. However, in about 20 percent of children this age, it overreacts and creates excess fear and anxiety within the child.[16]

Children this age also cue off their parents' emotions. If Carla's parents become anxious when she starts crying, it validates her fear and creates a memory for the hippocampus to draw upon next time. Over time, this creates a cycle and ultimately leads to irrational fears that are not easily dissuaded. However, if Carla's parents help her to calm and aren't overly emotional in the process, it helps Carla learn the skills needed to modulate intense emotions like fear.

Middle Childhood (Six to Eleven)

The years between ages six and eleven are fairly stable years for children, with their growth happening in a slow and steady fashion. They have developed the ability to care for their basic needs, which increases their self-esteem. Internally, their brains continue to develop and allow them to perform increasingly complex thought processes. The connections between different regions of the brain strengthen, and hubs—areas where large numbers of axons meet—begin to develop.[17] The prefrontal cortex begins to mature, which allows them to begin planning and evaluating. During this stage, children also develop the ability to selectively attend to one stimulus while ignoring other things happening at the same time.[18] Additionally, some brain functions become automated. This happens when a sequence of thoughts and actions is repeated until the neurons fire automatically, without needing conscious thought to trigger their firing.

Communication

As children progress through middle childhood, they begin to understand and appropriately utilize metaphors, jokes, and puns.[19] This new learning can create an endless stream of knock-knock jokes that test parents' patience. The ability to adjust vocabulary to unique contexts also begins to develop during middle childhood, allowing ten-year-old Nathan to talk more formally to a teacher than to his friends. Shy or anxious children may struggle to switch between context and tend to err on the side of using one form of communication regardless of the situation.

Learning and Memory

Piaget labeled the learning patterns of middle childhood *concrete operational thought* to emphasize the ability to use logical processes within concrete situations—situations grounded in what is tangible, observable, and real—but not in abstract or theoretical situations.

Middle childhood is characterized by curiosity and a desire to explore and learn. When this desire is fed, it gives children more tangible, observable experiences to utilize when making decisions. They have an ever-increasing ability to take information learned in one situation and apply it effectively in other similar situations. While Liza had limited ability to decide how she wanted to go about learning a new skill as a preschooler, as she enters middle childhood she will begin developing *metacognition*, the ability to step back and create a strategy for learning something.[20]

While younger children rely almost exclusively on the morality of adults to determine what is right and wrong, during middle childhood children begin developing and utilizing their own sense of morality.[21] As this autonomous morality develops, children begin seeing multiple dimensions to problems and different ways of applying social and moral rules. They no longer automatically see authority figures as right or obedience as the appropriate response in all situations. They also develop the ability to step into the shoes of another, having empathy for what the individual might be feeling and allowing this empathy to influence their decisions.

Emotions

Prior to middle childhood, children focus on learning to name and manage emotions with the help of others. During middle childhood, their focus shifts slightly. Children develop more independence and focus more on their sense of who they are combined with their sense of how others perceive them. During this phase of development, children spend a lot of emotional energy developing their self-concept, or "their ideas about themselves in terms of their intelligence, personality, abilities, gender, and ethnic background."[22] Developmental psychologist Erik Erikson describes this as the *industry versus inferiority stage*.[23] Across cultures, children in this age range are eager to learn and explore. If a child frequently masters new tasks they attempt, they develop a sense of competence that feeds a healthy self-concept. However, if a child perceives themselves as unsuccessful at mastering new concepts or believes others see them as unsuccessful, they internalize this and see themselves as inferior to their peer group. Part of the data used to draw their conclusions comes from their developing ability to compare themselves to others.[24] Middle childhood remains a time of relying almost exclusively upon concrete, tangible experiences. Concepts like kindness or generosity don't influence a child's self-concept nearly as much as whether they can run the fastest, get the most questions right on their math test, or have the longest hair.[25]

During infancy and early childhood, children rely upon others to manage their interpretation and response to events happening within the world around them, but in middle childhood they begin autonomously interpreting events. If Emanuel concludes negative things happening in the world around him occur because of either who he is or something he's done, his ability to develop *resilience*—the capacity to overcome and adapt after stress or adversity—is negatively impacted. Conversely, if Emanuel sees himself as able to control his *reaction* to stressful events rather than control *if* these events occur, he'll develop a healthy locus of control and resiliency. Emanuel's interpretation of the events he encounters, combined with his ability to solve problems and the support of his family and community, contribute to the development of healthy resiliency capacities.[26]

Middle childhood is where mental illness is often first diagnosed. Attention deficit hyperactivity disorder, conduct disorder, depression, and anxiety are frequently identified for the first time during this phase of development. Most adults find it difficult to fathom a seven- or eight-year-old having a mental illness. However, studies show as many as one in six children between the ages of six and seventeen have a diagnosable mental illness, and nearly half of these children do not receive treatment.[27] Even more alarming, according to the National Institute of Mental Health, "half of all mental health disorders show first signs before a person turns 14 years old."[28] As with any illness, when children have untreated mental illness, it is difficult for them to engage in the learning processes appropriate for their age. This makes it imperative to identify and appropriately treat mental illnesses.

Adolescence (Eleven to Nineteen)

The only development phase with a greater amount of change and more radical types of changes than adolescence is infancy. Use of the term *adolescence* to describe the distinct period of development between middle childhood and adulthood emerged by the end of the nineteenth century and was described by psychologist G. Stanley Hall as a period of "storm and stress."[29] Physically, this stage of development is marked by an increase in hormones leading to the onset of puberty. With the increase in hormones, the sexual organs and accompanying sexual feelings begin to develop. Myelination and maturation, occurring within the limbic system and other instinctual and emotional areas up to this point, become more focused on regions of the brain where reflection and analysis occur. The prefrontal cortex is developing but remains limited in its connections and ability to consistently remain engaged.[30] This means teens can understand the consequences of decisions better than their younger counterparts. However, the disparity in development between the limbic system and prefrontal cortex leaves adolescents experiencing intense emotions and impulses that are relatively unchecked by caution or the ability to engage in long-term planning. Additionally, the limbic system finds loud music, fast cars, and mind-altering substances compelling, while the pre-frontal cortex requires time and energy to generate an accurate understanding of the long-term consequences of engaging in what the limbic system finds compelling. Adolescents' well-developed limbic system allows them to have extremely fast reaction times, which enhances their athletic ability. Overall, adolescents develop what looks like an adult body, but their brain cannot function in all the ways adult brains function.

Communication

Adolescent communication is marked by an expanded ability to discuss, read, and write about abstract ideas; justify viewpoints; and engage in negotiation and persuasion (especially when parents set limits they don't like). Adolescents become skilled at adapting communication to fit their audience and at asking and answering questions contingent upon information they receive from individuals they are communicating with.[31] They combine this ability with an increasing awareness and utilization of nonverbal responses and slang vocabulary to effectively maintain connection and show affiliation with particular peer groups.

Learning and Memory

The adolescent brain is capable of intuitive and analytical reasoning. *Intuitive reasoning* relies upon instinct and gut reactions, so it happens rapidly and relies upon what "feels right." In contrast, *analytical reasoning* relies upon logical and rational analysis, which involves managing feelings and taking time to look at a situation through multiple lenses. While adolescents develop the capacity to do both, intuitive reasoning happens rapidly and has stronger feelings associated with it; therefore it tends to dominate adolescent thought. As synaptic growth continues within the brain, adolescents develop what Piaget called *formal operational thought*, the ability to consider ideas and theories of what might happen "if." When Joe utilizes formal operational thought, he considers multiple outcomes and weighs the pros and cons of all potential choices. As a result of this ability to think hypothetically, adolescents tend to become critical of everyone and everything as they think through what "should" have happened or what "could" happen. They question authority figures and begin to forge their own standards and beliefs that often endure into adulthood.

While they begin developing an understanding of what could happen in the future, they also operate under the "invincibility fable." Adolescents believe they won't die until their predestined time to die, so they can do whatever they want prior to that time and it won't produce death.[32] Because her prefrontal cortex is just developing, fifteen-year-old Natalie can sit with her parents at dinner and provide insightful, logical reasons why it would be detrimental and unwise to engage in activities like using drugs. However, when Natalie is approached by a peer at a party later the same evening and asked to use, the better developed pleasure-seeking centers of her brain respond more rapidly than her prefrontal cortex. This, combined with the invincibility fable, may cause Natalie to make decisions at the party that she previously told her parents, youth leader, and other adults she would never make.

Emotions

Adolescence is characterized by *egocentrism* and intense emotions. If you look back at the description of the toddler years, you will see this same theme. The main difference is that teens *can* see things from another point of view, while toddlers are incapable of doing this. The hallmark of teenage egocentrism is seeing oneself as center stage with everyone else forming the audience, watching and critiquing their every move. This view of the world leaves teens feeling incredibly self-conscious while also seeing themselves as more (or less) unique, special, and liked than everyone around them.[33] They want to fit in with everyone around them while simultaneously wanting to feel special and unique (talk about distressing!). Their self-consciousness also leaves them feeling everyone else's behavior is a judgment of them, which, in turn, leads to conflicting thoughts and feelings about their parents, friends, self, and future.

The adolescent brain's underdeveloped prefrontal cortex causes emotions to rule over behavior. Teen brains experience heightened arousal in the reward centers, causing them to seek excitement and pleasure, especially if the pleasure involves peer admiration.[34] This can be especially evident when teens gather in groups. When eighteen-year-old Brian's peers are present, he finds himself taking dramatic risks he wouldn't consider doing alone—like drag racing on back streets—that are both socially rewarding and emotionally pleasurable.[35] Teenagers also have higher levels of *cortisol*, which causes them to react with anger or other intense emotions more quickly than adults.[36] These emotions are intense and often grounded in the teens' perception of what happened, what the teens believe others might be thinking or feeling about what happened, or what the teens believe others are thinking about them rather than being grounded in reality.[37]

Erikson describes the tasks associated with adolescence as *identity versus role confusion*. Adolescents question and tear apart the goals and values of their parents to determine which of these they are willing to internalize as they forge their own identity. This results in a dramatic increase in conflict between parents and teens, but this questioning of goals and values and the ensuing conflict is necessary for teens to develop their own sense of self. Until adolescence, parents function as the center of the child's world, much like the sun functions as the center of the solar system. The gravitational pull of the sun keeps the planets in orbit much like the beliefs, values, and behaviors of parents keep their child's life functioning in healthy ways. During adolescence, teens begin to break out of this orbit. This process requires considerable effort on their part.

While teens don't want their life to center around their parents, they recognize the need for adult influences in their life and often choose another trusted adult to turn to for information and guidance. While this sometimes feels threatening to parents, teens need a teacher, coach, neighbor, family member, or youth ministry leader to be an "expert" in their life as they begin to function independently of their parents.[38] While parents are no longer seen as experts, their support and approval continue to be immensely important to teens (although they'll adamantly deny needing or wanting it). In addition to trusted adults, teens rely heavily upon peers as they navigate the changes in their world. Although not the case, at times it can seem as though relationships with and opinions of peers are the only things that matter in a teen's life.[39] As teens establish their sense of identity, they commit to a set of goals and begin to consistently live out of those values as they pursue these goals.

Studies show about 23 percent of adolescents meet criteria for a mental illness.[40] The changes within hormones, body structure, mental processing, and emotions experienced during adolescence heighten teens' vulnerability to developing a mental illness. Suicide is the third leading cause of death among adolescents[41]—partly due to the combination of volatile teen emotions, the invincibility fable, and the impulsive decision-making processes associated with the teen years. While 75 percent of mental illnesses develop prior to age twenty-four,[42] effective treatments exist, and it is crucial to help teens identify when they are struggling with a mental illness and to get appropriate treatment so they can effectively recover and engage their lives fully.

Applying What You Learned

At the end of each chapter is a list of questions to help you identify specific things to consider as you work to help your child effectively manage the anxiety in their life.

As you conclude this chapter, consider:

1. What characteristics in the sections you read apply to your child?
2. What characteristics in the sections you read don't fit your child?
3. What things do you want to remember about how your child communicates, learns, and feels differently than an adult?
4. What things do you do that might not be effective, given your child's stage of development?
5. What things can you do to increase your effectiveness, given your child's stage of development?

TWO

Normal Childhood Development or Anxiety?

Given the uniqueness of each stage of childhood development, it makes sense that the fears, experiences of anxiety, and ways a child expresses anxiety vary depending upon the age of the child. Also, just as some types of anxiety are perfectly normal within adults, healthy children have things they are afraid of that vary by age.

Anxiety exists along a continuum from appropriate and healthy to a mental illness that requires treatment to prevent it from interfering in normal childhood development. Anxiety exhibits itself in multiple ways, many factors contribute to its presence, and there is no known "cure." However, there are resources and skills to effectively manage anxiety. It doesn't have to interfere with your child's ability to engage in the normal activities necessary for them to grow and develop into a healthy adult.

Part of the difficulty associated with anxiety stems from how the word is used. The same word is used to denote both a healthy response to an upcoming test and a serious mental illness that can prevent a child from living their life in a healthy way. Imagine if the word *diabetic* could mean either your child is experiencing a sugar rush after overindulging in Christmas candy or your child has a serious medical illness requiring you to administer insulin immediately. We would never think of using the same term to describe both! However, *anxiety* is a catchall description for almost every kind of worry or anxious thought.

Anxiety is a term much like the term *blood sugar*; it describes certain thoughts, feelings, and physical sensations just as blood sugar describes certain chemicals within the body. Everyone has blood sugar, and it is considered normal if it stays within a certain range. When it leaves the "normal" range, it is a medical condition requiring treatment for the individual involved to return to health. Similarly, all children experience anxiety, and it is healthy if it stays within a certain range. When anxiety exceeds the "normal" range, it becomes a medical condition that requires treatment just like any other medical condition for the child to return to health.

Healthy Anxiety

Children are born with the ability to physiologically respond when placed in stressful situations. Even the smallest infants, when startled by a loud sound, will gasp slightly, involuntarily jerk, and begin crying. This physical response helps them adapt to the stressor and gain the attention of someone who can make sure they are safe and protected. This healthy anxiety helps ensure the infant remains safe amid a dangerous world.

Healthy anxiety triggers what is commonly referred to as "fight-flight-freeze," a set of automatic responses designed to help people effectively cope with perceived danger. Suppose three teens are riding together in a car and the driver decides to attempt a curve marked as 35 mph at 55 mph. Everyone initially laughs, but as the car begins to feel out of control midcurve, the passengers yell at the driver to "Stop it or you're going to kill us!" (fight). Contrast that with an unknown, gregarious woman moving toward a toddler and saying, "Come here and give me a hug," as the toddler retreats behind his father's leg (flight). Alternatively, when a three-year-old approaches an escalator, she stops cold at the bottom and refuses to budge as her mom tugs on her arm in an attempt to get her to step on (freeze). When children encounter things their brains perceive as potentially dangerous, their brains rapidly change. Depending upon the age of the child, these changes will exhibit themselves differently, making it vital to remember what is true of your child developmentally when your child becomes frightened.

The prefrontal cortex (which isn't fully developed until the midtwenties) is the part of your child's brain that

- makes decisions
- plans complex behaviors
- sorts out conflicting thoughts
- determines what is good and bad
- makes sure choices move an individual toward their goals
- determines whether thoughts are socially appropriate to act upon
- determines long-term consequences of behaviors

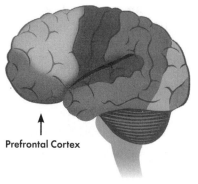

Prefrontal Cortex

When your child encounters perceived danger, their prefrontal cortex is bypassed, and their body draws upon their limbic system to respond. The limbic system, located in the middle of the head, is composed of several parts that are always on alert to identify potential harm. It functions much like a home security system—when it senses danger, it sounds the alarm and causes your child's body to kick into high alert. When that alarm goes off,

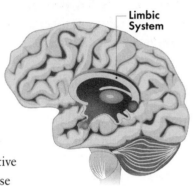

Limbic System

- the heart races
- breathing becomes shallow
- muscles become tense, making movements jerky
- the startle response becomes intensely sensitive to any movement or noise

These changes happen without any conscious thought and physically prepare the body to fight off the attack, run away from the threat, or freeze and hope it will go away. The fight-flight-freeze response is necessary, healthy, and allows your child to react quickly and as appropriately as they can, given their age, when danger approaches.

The Worry Zone

The reactions we've talked about so far are instinctual and happen without conscious thought. However, as the brain develops, so does the ability to worry. Infants and even young toddlers do not worry, but from the older toddler years on, children can and do worry. *Worry* can be defined as persistently thinking about problems, fears, or concerns out of fear something bad has happened or could happen. Worry differs from the healthy anxiety we previously discussed in that it is driven by internal thought processes rather than external stimuli. If six-year-old Pauline incessantly questions her mother with "what if" scenarios about strangers they pass in the shopping mall, this represents worry. Worry is a learned pattern used in an attempt to cope with unknowns. It is born out of the child's belief that if they think enough about everything that "might" happen, it will ensure nothing bad occurs. Couple this with the fact children don't know what will and won't harm or kill them or the people they love, and you create a natural breeding ground for worry.

Children seem to have healthy anxiety and worry about the same sorts of things at each of the different development stages.

Birth to Two Years

At this stage, your child will have healthy anxiety about the following sorts of things:

- *Loud noises.* Young children do not know what sort of danger the loud noise may represent.
- *Unfamiliar objects.* Young children have no frame of reference to determine if something they have never encountered before may be dangerous. When something is unknown, it triggers their body's limbic system, and their hippocampus has no memories with which to dampen this response.
- *Strangers.* This fear develops after four months of age and is designed to keep your child next to caregivers who can protect them.

Early Childhood

During this phase, most of your child's reactions will represent healthy anxiety, but you may see worry begin to develop. Typical things creating anxiety or worry within this phase include:

- *Imaginary creatures and costumes.* Children in this phase don't have a clear understanding of what is real and what isn't. Imaginary and pretend creatures (monsters, ghosts, and so forth) pose real danger in their minds. Additionally, when people wear costumes, the costume appears real and creates a real threat in the child's mind.

- *The dark.* Because children operate in a concrete fashion at this age, when they can't see what is there, they easily become scared of what might be there and need reassurance that they are safe.

- *Animals, insects, blood, elevators, and other new experiences.* Because children in this phase are not sure of what will and won't harm them, new things or even new variations of things they have already seen (a new dog they have never seen before) can create anxiety.

- *Parents leaving.* Children at this phase recognize they need their parents for survival and are attached to their parents. They also operate based upon what is tangibly present and don't have a sense of time—both of which make it easy for them to become fearful that when parents leave, they may not return.

- *Death.* During this phase, children often become aware of the idea of death. However, since death, aging, and illness are abstract concepts and they are unable to think in the abstract, they don't know how old someone must be to die and what it means when someone dies. Their tangible understanding of death is someone leaving, so this makes them fearful people they love and/or depend upon may die.

Middle Childhood

Developmentally, this is the stage where the prefrontal cortex—the area of the brain responsible for evaluating and planning—is developing. This ability to evaluate and plan contributes to the fact middle childhood is the developmental stage where worry sometimes begins to dominate a child's life. The typical things creating worry for children at this age include:

- *Dangers around them.* Children this age cannot yet differentiate between what is likely to happen and what is unlikely to happen. As a result, they fear storms, burglars, kidnappers, illness, and getting hurt. They are aware these are dangerous but cannot yet differentiate how dangerous each is to them at any given moment.

- *Death.* As children gain an understanding that things like not taking care of yourself or not feeling well often precede death, they become fearful parents who aren't taking care of themselves or family members who are ill may die. They may even become fearful they will die if they are ill.

- *Failure.* At this age, children are evaluating themselves against their peers and want to be successful. This can cause them to begin worrying about not being successful in ways they didn't in the past.

- *Friendships.* In middle childhood, a lot of energy is focused on self-concept. Learning social rules, finding ways to fit in, and being part of a group are part of this process, and many children in this age range worry about these things.

Adolescence

Children in this developmental stage are highly focused on what "could" or "should" happen and also understand abstract concepts. These factors, combined with a shift in focus from their parents to their peers as the center of their lives, make it common for adolescents to develop worries about these sorts of things:

- *Appearance.* Teenagers are aware their bodies are changing. Simultaneously, they perceive themselves to be center stage with everyone critiquing them. This makes it common for them to fear something is "wrong" with them and to become excessively worried about things like the zit they are sure everyone can see a mile away.

- *Relationships.* Teens want to be special and attractive enough to be chosen by a romantic partner. They also want to belong to a group, and they fear not being chosen by the peer group they wish to identify with. Once chosen, they tend to fear doing something that could cause them to become excluded or ostracized.

- *Future events.* Teens want to be successful as adults and become fearful they may not "have what it takes." They also worry about things that might happen to them or to people they care about in the future. They simultaneously feel mature enough to be an adult and childlike enough to fear they won't be able to function in the adult world.

- *Issues.* Teens have the ability to create gray areas in their life, but they still tend to see issues in black-and-white terms and can spend a lot of time worrying about injustice, inequality, and things that feel unfair in their life and in the world at large.

Worry creates a feeling of uneasiness and results in being overly concerned about a situation or potential problem. Worry forces your child's mind and body to remain vigilant for potential threats. When they are in this on-alert state, it is difficult for them to focus on what is happening around them or to think about much of anything other than the worry.

The primary difference between healthy anxiety and worry is its focus. Worry is focused on the things your child fears *might* happen. Both healthy anxiety and worry trigger the same chemical reactions physiologically. In both cases the body gears up to fight, flee, or freeze. While you want your teen to have this response if a car veers into their lane as they are driving, it is hard for them to get to sleep at night if their body is in this state. Worry's focus on what might happen keeps your child's body on alert and controlled by the limbic system, making logical thought and learning (which occur in other regions of the brain) difficult.

Fight-Flight-Freeze Causes

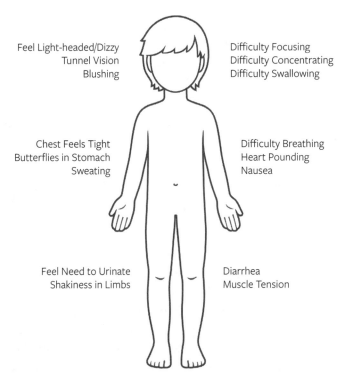

Feel Light-headed/Dizzy
Tunnel Vision
Blushing

Difficulty Focusing
Difficulty Concentrating
Difficulty Swallowing

Chest Feels Tight
Butterflies in Stomach
Sweating

Difficulty Breathing
Heart Pounding
Nausea

Feel Need to Urinate
Shakiness in Limbs

Diarrhea
Muscle Tension

Both worry and healthy anxiety cause the limbic system to release stress hormones like cortisol into your child's body. As those hormones enter the bloodstream, they produce the responses you see in the diagram. While these responses are helpful when facing danger, they are not intended to linger. Worry often persists over time, and when the body is stressed in this way, it is negatively impacted. The American Medical Association has stated stress is the basic cause of more than 60 percent of all human illnesses and diseases.[1] Over time, the stress of ongoing unresolved anxiety and worry adversely affects virtually every system in your child's body.

The stress produced by worry can be harmful for your child emotionally, spiritually, and physically and is what Paul refers to in Scripture when he says, "Do not be anxious about anything" (Phil. 4:6). Unlike healthy anxiety that is necessary, or mental illnesses that children don't cause, worry is a way of reacting to the unknowns in the world. It is normal for children to have fears and to worry about things their young brains are not yet developed enough to fully understand. However, they don't have to end up becoming adults who describe themselves as "a born worrier." You play a key role in helping your child learn healthy coping skills for dealing with the unknowns of their life without worrying.

Anxiety Disorders

Every child is born with healthy anxiety. Children naturally develop the capacity to worry, and for some children, this becomes an integral part of daily life. A subset of children move beyond this to develop a diagnosable anxiety-related mental illness. According to the studies identifying the frequency of mental illness in children, 7.1 percent (or approximately 4.4 million) of children ages three to seventeen have a diagnosed anxiety disorder.[2] Research also shows the number of children ages six to seventeen who have been diagnosed with an anxiety disorder rose from 5.5 percent in 2007 to 6.4 percent in 2012.[3] Even more alarming is the number of these children who don't receive treatment. Of the approximately 4.4 million children who have a diagnosed anxiety disorder, only 59.3 percent (2.6 million) receive treatment.[4] This means 1.8 million children have a serious and debilitating illness that is left untreated. How can this be?

Until the MRI was invented in the 1970s and the Functional MRI in the 1980s, scientists and doctors didn't have technology that allowed them to determine how the brain functioned. Prior to this, most of what was known about the brain was conjecture mixed with what could be learned through autopsies. Without evidence to show what happens when the brain becomes ill, doctors were left with little they could do to treat children struggling with symptoms we would now define as anxiety disorders.

The symptoms of anxiety disorders also look similar to what happens when one worries. With no way of differentiating mental illness from worry, family members, clergy, and even doctors prescribed "better parenting," "stronger faith," "just stop it," and "just think about something else" to children and adults struggling with what was labeled a moral or parental failing.

While our understanding of the human brain has expanded considerably, the stigma of having a mental illness has not receded at the same rate. This stigma sometimes makes parents fearful about seeking treatment for their child. Additionally, it is often inconceivable to adults that children can develop mental illness, so parents explain away symptoms. These two factors combine to create a reluctance in parents to seek assistance when they have a child struggling with anxiety.

The medical term *disorder* is used to describe this grouping of illnesses and refers to a pattern of disruptions in how the body normally functions. This means anxiety disorders are illnesses characterized by specific patterns in how the body malfunctions. Like any medical disorder, there are things that make an anxiety disorder better or worse, but anxiety disorders are not caused by moral failings, defiance, or lack of willpower. They are medical illnesses just like diabetes, cardiac arrhythmias, and seizures. This is an important fact for you, as parents, to know and to reinforce with your child if they struggle with an anxiety disorder.

Since anxiety disorders share some features with worry and healthy anxiety, parents may find it difficult to determine if their child's experience falls within the "normal" range or is something more serious requiring treatment. The difference is not necessarily in the content of what your child is upset about. Rather, it is in the level of distress this reaction is causing within your child and within their life. Children often are unable to articulate what they are feeling physically or emotionally, but they act different behaviorally when they are struggling. The following behavioral changes should serve as "red flags" for parents, indicating something outside the norm may be going on:

- worries or fears that persist for more than a couple of weeks
- physical issues like headaches, upset stomachs, diarrhea, difficulty getting to sleep at night, nightmares, or other complaints of illness that persists over time and doesn't seem to have an identifiable cause
- a pattern of thinking negatively or assuming bad things are going to happen
- frequent requests for reassurance (promise me you'll sit right outside my room, promise me I'm okay, promise me you'll go with me)
- frequent anxious inquiries about "what if" and an inability to be satisfied with the answers you give
- irritability or anger with self or others when things do not go the way your child perceives they should
- self-criticism and/or being extremely worried about what others think of them or the things they are doing
- refusing to engage in age-appropriate activities (going to school, doing things with friends, trying new things)
- behavior that frequently interferes with your family's ability to function normally (such as avoiding things or making requests for reassurance)
- statements about wishing they didn't exist, wishing they were dead, or wanting to kill themselves

Anxiety disorders can be thought of in three groups: reactions to something specific, reactions to trauma, and general reactions without a specific trigger. These are not scientific groups but do provide a framework for this conversation.

Anxiety Disorders Triggered by Something Specific

The American Psychiatric Association, which identifies the criteria used to diagnose mental illnesses, includes the following diagnoses for anxiety that fit into the category of being a reaction to something specific.

Separation Anxiety Disorder

Most children outgrow the normal anxiety around separation from caregivers somewhere around age three. When a child's anxiety about separating from caregivers persists beyond this, it can be a sign of a separation anxiety disorder. Children struggling with a separation anxiety disorder worry excessively about separating from or losing loved ones.[5]

Social Anxiety Disorder

Social anxiety disorder is connected to being in either a specific social setting or all social settings. Children suffering from this disorder want to be in social situations, but their fear is so intense they avoid them.[6]

Selective Mutism

Selective mutism is an anxiety disorder related to being in social situations. Even though they possess the ability to speak, children with selective mutism have a pattern of consistently failing to speak in social situations where they would be expected to (like at school), although they do speak in other situations. This failure to speak interferes with their ability to function normally within school or social situations.[7]

Specific Phobias

Specific phobias develop as a reaction to something such as blood or spiders. Children struggling with this disorder experience intense, unreasonable fear either when they are in the presence of the feared object or in anticipation of being in the presence of the object.[8]

Obsessive-Compulsive Disorder

Children struggling with obsessive-compulsive disorder (OCD) experience intrusive thoughts about something specific, such as becoming contaminated by germs or harming someone. These intrusive thoughts are highly anxiety-provoking and distressing, so children perform rituals in an attempt to manage the thoughts and the anxiety they produce. Children often attempt to hide their rituals from others, causing them to isolate in unhealthy ways.[9]

Agoraphobia

Children with agoraphobia fear being in places where it might be difficult or embarrassing to leave, so they avoid such situations or require someone to go with them as a companion to help them face the fear.[10]

Anxiety Disorders Triggered by Trauma

Trauma reactions occur when a child experiences or is exposed to a situation that feels traumatic to them. What may feel traumatic to one child may not feel traumatic to another. Also, what children experience as traumatic is different from what is traumatic for adults. For example, a child may watch a horror movie and experience it as trauma while an adult would know it is not real and would not be traumatized. Similarly, two children may be exposed to the same horror movie and one will experience it as trauma while the other is not particularly bothered by it. Many factors play a role in determining whether something will be experienced as trauma, including how many previous traumas the child has experienced,

Acute Stress Disorder and Post-Traumatic Stress Disorder

When a child is exposed to a traumatic event, they may develop an acute stress disorder or post-traumatic stress disorder (PTSD), causing them to reexperience the event repeatedly; avoid activities, people, or places connected with the event; and experience extreme distress when exposed to anything reminding them of the event.[11] The diagnosis of acute stress disorder applies if symptoms occur within the first four weeks after the event and resolve within the same one-month period. PTSD is the diagnosis for these same symptoms if the event occurred over a month ago and the symptoms persist. A child with PTSD may experience a sense of detachment from themselves, their surroundings, or their emotions—especially when reexperiencing the traumatic event or encountering something connected to the event.[12]

Anxiety Disorders without a Specific Trigger

Two anxiety disorders are not triggered by an object or experience and are more pervasive and unpredictable as a result.

Panic Attacks

A panic attack is a period of intense fear that develops seemingly "out of nowhere" and causes the child to experience:

- chest pain, palpitations, or tachycardia
- chills, hot flashes, or sweating
- disconnection from reality or from self
- fear of losing control
- dizziness, light-headedness, or faintness
- feelings of choking, shortness of breath, or feelings of smothering
- trembling or shaking[13]

These symptoms peak within ten minutes and then slowly dissipate. They are intensely distressing, and often children struggling with these symptoms believe they are dying.

Generalized Anxiety Disorder

Unlike children with specific phobias, where something identifiable creates anxiety, children with a generalized anxiety disorder are simply anxious about many things, most of the time, for at least six months. They find it difficult, and sometimes impossible, to control their fears and also find themselves worrying and feeling restless, keyed up, or on edge to the point they may be unable to get to or stay asleep.[14]

Depending upon their age, children struggling with any of the anxiety disorders discussed may or may not know their fear is unrealistic. Either way, they are unable to stop the fear. It is so intense it interferes with their ability to function in healthy ways at school, at home, or in peer relationships.

☰ *Applying What You Learned*

Anxiety exists along a continuum from healthy anxiety to debilitating illness. While I am not a fan of parents attempting to diagnose their child, it can be helpful to evaluate where you believe your child falls on the continuum. If you look back over the past six months of your child's life and find most of the times your child was anxious were related to external events, the anxiety did not interfere with their ability to function in healthy ways, and

Healthy Anxiety   Worry Zone   Anxiety Disorders

the anxiety dissipated when the event passed, then most of your child's anxiety was probably within the healthy range.

You might conclude your child falls into the worry zone if you look back over the past six months and find those months were filled with anticipation of potential problems or negative events and attempts to prevent bad things from happening—even when they should have been sleeping or enjoying other activities. Even worry exists on a continuum from mildly annoying to interfering with a child's ability to live life in a healthy manner.

For some parents, as you read the list of red flags and the various anxiety disorders, you found yourself repeatedly saying, "My child does this." Please know: this doesn't necessarily mean your child has an anxiety disorder. Instead, I would suggest you may want to explore what this means with your child's doctor, a counselor, or a psychiatrist, as these people are trained to diagnose and treat anxiety disorders. Seek assistance in determining what is going on for your child, because anxiety disorders have symptoms similar to other medical conditions, making it tricky and important to accurately determine what is causing your child's symptoms.

Whether you identified your child as having healthy anxiety or found yourself wondering if they might have an anxiety disorder, the rest of this book will help you understand both what causes them to feel anxious and what things you can do to help them manage the anxiety they are experiencing.

THREE

Helping Children Understand They Are Not Their Anxiety

Anxiety and worry are abstract concepts—you can't see them like you see an apple sitting on the counter. While most adults can conceptualize abstract concepts, children and many adolescents cannot. However, children and the adults in their world need to be able to conceptualize anxiety. Unless a child has a way to think about anxiety as a tangible thing, it is difficult for them to understand they are not defined by the anxiety they experience. When children come to counseling, they frequently describe the problem as, "I'm anxious." This type of statement defines the child by the illness they're experiencing. When anxiety becomes part of a child's identity, it makes it hard for them to let go of the anxiety without feeling they are losing who they are as an individual. In this chapter, we will look at ways to help children conceptualize anxiety as something separate from who they are. We will also identify the different areas influencing the development of anxiety disoders as well as how anxiety is experienced.

Externalizing Anxiety

Children often lack language skills to describe emotions or physical feelings. This makes it essential not to rely solely upon language to help children communicate what they are experiencing. Children express what they are feeling through their play, their art, and their behaviors. We want to capitalize upon this to help them develop ways to describe what they experience and to externalize anxiety instead of seeing it as a part of their identity. There are many ways to do this. As a child, my daughter loved music, dance, and all things Disney. As a middle-school student, my son was enthralled with *Lord of the Rings* and *Star Wars*. If I had asked my eight-year-old daughter to describe the anxiety she was feeling, she would probably have told me it was Ursula from *The Little Mermaid*—always present and unexpectedly able to become larger than life and make everyone cower. My middle-school son, however, might have chosen the Eye of Sauron to represent anxiety—vigilant and intent upon invading his life, stealing what he valued, and destroying him.

What is important in both examples is that the anxiety takes a tangible form, has qualities of its own, and is outside of the child. I've had children describe anxiety as a variety of different animals, people, characters, vehicles, or substances. Your child needs to create the picture of what anxiety is in their life, and the picture must be meaningful to them. A small child might describe anxiety as a ferocious barking dog, while an adolescent might describe it as a tornado rolling through their life.

As a parent, your role is to develop genuine curiosity around what your child is experiencing. Consider asking questions like these:

- Can you draw me a picture of what it feels like inside when you feel scared? Tell me about your picture.
- If your feelings were a cartoon or movie character, what character would they be? How is what you feel similar to this character?

- Is there someone or something similar to what you feel when you are scared? How is this person/thing similar to your feeling?

Questions like these begin to create an avenue for children to share what they feel when they are upset and scared without having to rely solely upon using words to describe their experience.

As children pick a way of describing what they are feeling, don't criticize or correct what they describe. It would be easy to tell my son his anxiety couldn't really be as big or powerful as Sauron, but this would minimize and invalidate his experience. Instead, I need to validate that having feelings as big and scary as Sauron with all his armies must feel incredibly overwhelming at times.

It can also be helpful to give the anxiety a name. When I work with adolescents struggling with eating disorders, we call their eating disorder "Ed." By naming it, we externalize it and have ways of talking about Ed as separate from them. For purposes of this book, we are going to describe anxiety as a lion named Aggie. Lions are usually the largest and scariest animals children know. Children describe lions as very scary and hard to ignore when they roar. They are powerful animals, and if you meet an uncaged lion, when the lion roars or starts moving toward you, it is important to run so you don't get hurt. Only when you are standing outside of the lion's cage is it safe to be around a lion. However, lion trainers have special skills, and they can be inside a cage with a lion without being afraid or getting hurt. In fact, lion trainers can be in the cage with a lion and teach it to do what they want it to do, instead of letting the lion control what the trainer does.

Anxiety is the scariest feeling most children have ever experienced. When children feel anxious, the feeling is so intense and consuming it feels like it might kill them, so all they want to do is get away from this feeling and whatever creates it. For children, anxiety, like a lion, is to be avoided whenever possible. Most children experience anxiety as a wild lion with no cage and no trainer—it's on the prowl, and they just want to stay away from it. However, they can become really good lion trainers who learn they don't need to be afraid of Aggie the lion (anxiety) and learn how to control Aggie instead of having Aggie control them.

What Causes Anxiety/Worry?

After your child develops an understanding of anxiety separate from who they are, you can then begin to help them see how different factors influence whether anxiety shows up in their life. Both worry and anxiety disorders have different factors that influence if they develop, when they develop, and how they are best treated. You and your child can develop a holistic understanding of the factors influencing the development and effective treatment of anxiety disorders. You, as a parent, can begin by developing an understanding of the different factors influencing anxiety, and then learning ways to begin talking with your child about this.

Systems Theory

As medical research expands and shows connections between health and a broad variety of factors, theories for what "causes" and "cures" illnesses are being replaced by another idea: *systems theory*. A system is composed of interrelated and interdependent parts. For example, your digestive system is composed of all the different organs involved in eating, digesting, and eliminating food.

Your child's life is composed of their body's internal systems and all the external systems they are part of. Your child is part of a family, a school, a faith community, a neighborhood, extracurricular activities, and so on. Each of these systems is intricately connected to your child, and your child is connected to each system. Each system is simultaneously independent (it performs a unique set of functions) and interdependent (every system is surrounded by and influenced by other systems). Systems theory posits when you change one part of any system, it affects other parts of that system and all other associated systems. Biological, psychological, social, and spiritual systems all contribute to the development of illnesses—including anxiety disorders—and need to be part of any effective, holistic treatment.

Let's look at each system separately first.

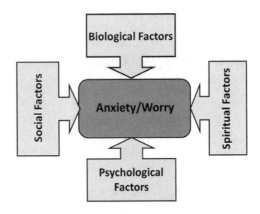

Biological Factors

Until recently, pediatricians worked primarily to label medical conditions correctly and identify medications that successfully treated each illness. While this enabled physicians to correctly identify illnesses, it failed to identify the different factors that contribute to the development of specific illnesses and need to be addressed to appropriately manage them. Organizations like the Centers for Disease Control (CDC) have done extensive research to help identify factors that influence who will develop certain illnesses and how the illness will affect their lives.

Research shows genetic predisposition plays a role in determining whether a child develops an anxiety disorder. However, genetics is only one piece of the picture. We are learning more about how diet, exercise, sleep, and the overall health of the child play a role in the development of anxiety disorders and in their effective treatment. No one factor, by itself, is solely responsible, but all must be taken into consideration to effectively provide treatment.

Psychological Factors

Substantial research has been conducted on the connection between the mind and the body. This research has shown chronic stress affects the immune system and creates issues within the gastrointestinal system. As the body of research expands, the impact of thought patterns on health is becoming clearer. While most of this research has been conducted on adults, studies show children's thoughts affect their health. The impact of childhood thought patterns like worry on physical health is typically underestimated by parents. A survey conducted in 2010 showed 20 percent of children ages eight to seventeen report worrying a great deal or a lot about things like doing well in school. Of these same children, 33 percent reported experiencing headaches within the last month and 44 percent reported difficulties with sleep. However, when the parents of these children were asked about it, only 3 percent reported believing their children were worrying a lot, only 13 percent of parents thought their children's headaches were related to worrying, and only 13 percent of parents believed their children were experiencing sleep difficulties.[1]

How children think about themselves and the world around them affects whether they will develop physical illness like headaches, stomach upset, and sleep difficulties. Their thoughts also affect (but don't control) if they develop an anxiety disorder, exacerbate an anxiety disorder, and help children effectively manage an anxiety disorder.

Social Factors

Recently, our understanding of factors contributing to the development of illness has expanded to include variables called *social determinants of health*. CDC research clearly shows conditions in a child's environment affect their health in the short and long term. Living in a safe neighborhood, having a family with enough resources to buy healthy foods, being able to attend a good school where they are taught in ways they learn best, and living in an environment where they feel safe and valued are all predictive of what illnesses a child will develop and how those illnesses progress.[2] Living with environmental stressors can contribute to anxiety disorders and impact a child's ability to cope with them.

Spiritual Factors

Spirituality and health were linked together from the beginning of recorded history until the Enlightenment period, and they have remained linked in many developing nations. Prior to the Enlightenment, physicians were often clergy. The intricate connection between faith and medicine wasn't always a good thing and sometimes led to horrendous practices like performing exorcisms on children to treat conditions like epilepsy. However, totally separating faith from medicine has created problems that have been just as devastating.

As research examining the influence of religion and spirituality on health has expanded, faith is consistently proving to play a vital role in the prevention and treatment of illness—including anxiety. A recent study of millennials across twenty-five countries showed those who attended church weekly were less likely to experience anxiety than those who didn't. Faith also contributes to adolescents having more hope and feeling less lonely and depressed.[3] Studies also show children with a faith background have better health than those without.[4] Faith affects the amount of anxiety experienced in stressful situations or when mistakes are made.[5]

Helping Children Understand Systems Theory

Children and adolescents want to feel some sense of control over what happens within their environment and within themselves. This, combined with their egocentric view of the world, often causes them to conclude they control things that aren't within their power or that they control nothing at all. This can be particularly true with anxiety. Children tend to either conclude the anxiety they experience is their fault and because they can't make it go away there is something flawed about them, or conclude they have no power over anxiety and are helpless victims under its reign of terror. Children need to understand that many different variables play a role in their feelings of worry and anxiety. Once they understand this, the next step is to help them see how they can influence each of these variables and, thus, affect the worry and anxiety they experience. Their understanding must be built from things children understand and can see. For the remainder of this chapter we'll explore ways to help children understand each of the areas influencing the worry and anxiety they experience. You can adapt these or use totally different examples that make more sense to your child.

Biological Factors

Aggie is a beautiful animal that runs fast and fearlessly plays. Aggie's trainer feeds him, keeps his cage warm and clean, and takes him out of his cage to run around and play every day. As long as his trainer does this, Aggie plays, enjoys his day, and does the tricks his trainer has taught him to do whenever his trainer asks him to. However, if Aggie's trainer forgets to feed Aggie for a couple of days, Aggie is going to get mighty hungry, and this is going to cause him to be really upset. If Aggie hasn't gotten to eat, all he can think about is how hungry he is. He is going to get scared he might die because he is so hungry. When Aggie sees his trainer, he is going to roar and roar and roar to try to get his trainer to see he needs to eat. Instead of listening to the trainer when he's asked to perform the tricks he's learned, Aggie is going to sit and roar and refuse to do anything the trainer says.

Our bodies are like Aggie, and we are the trainer. If we take care of our bodies just like the trainer takes care of Aggie, our bodies will listen to us and do what we ask of them. However, if we don't take good care of our bodies, they are going to "roar" at us, just like Aggie, to tell us something is wrong.

Additionally, some lions, like Mufasa from *The Lion King*, are not scared of many things. Other lions, like Simba, don't always know what they should be afraid of. Similarly, some of us have bodies that don't get scared and don't roar at us often while others have bodies that get scared and roar easily. Simba learned not to be afraid, just like we can teach our bodies not to be afraid quite so easily. We can do things to take care of our bodies, and this helps them to work well.

Psychological Factors

Aggie's trainer oversees teaching Aggie how to jump through the hoop he holds up. Aggie has never done this before, and neither has the trainer. As Aggie's trainer walks up to Aggie, the trainer thinks, *I'm not sure Aggie can do this. He has never jumped this high before. What if he misses the hoop and claws me with those massive claws?* As the trainer thinks this, his hand starts to shake a bit and his stomach starts to feel a little queasy. *Oh, no*, the trainer thinks. *This really is scary and I could get hurt.* The trainer then thinks of all the different ways Aggie could hurt him and all the different reasons Aggie might not be able to jump through the hoop. Pretty soon, Aggie's trainer is shaking all over as he looks at Aggie.

Aggie sees his trainer shaking and begins to fear something is wrong. He looks around and starts to roar, just in case something is out there trying to hurt him. Now both Aggie and the trainer are scared, and neither one of them can think about Aggie jumping through the hoop because they are focused on how scared they are.

The same is true with worry and anxiety. We often are faced with things we have never done before, like reading in front of the class or asking someone we like out on a date. When this happens, if we tell ourselves we aren't going to be able to do it because it's too scary and bad things might happen, we get really worried and scared. This makes it hard to even try to read aloud or walk up to that special someone and talk to them. In fact, it may even make us feel too scared to try at all. Every time we tell ourselves we can't do it or we are going to get hurt, we become more afraid and worried until eventually it is too scary to even think about trying the new activity.

Social Factors

Before Aggie came to live with the lion trainer, he lived in the wild and scary jungle. As he walked through the jungle, he was always afraid of being bitten by a poisonous snake. There wasn't much food around, so he worried about if he was going to have enough to eat. It was cold and rainy in the jungle, so he was also scared he wouldn't have a safe, dry place to sleep at night. When the lion trainer came to get him from the jungle, he scared Aggie, who had never seen a human before and wasn't sure if humans hurt lions. Even after the lion trainer took Aggie to live with him in a place where he didn't ever see snakes and had a warm cage full of clean straw to sleep in, Aggie still found himself afraid most of the time. It took Aggie a long time to trust that the lion trainer wouldn't hurt him and that his cage was a safe place to live.

Eventually, Aggie learned to trust that the lion trainer would keep Aggie safe, but it took him a long time, since he had lived in such a scary place for so long. The same is true with worry and anxiety. If we live in places that feel unsafe to us, or we're picked on and called names when we go to school, it's hard not to feel anxious and worried all the time. If we go to a new school or move to a safer neighborhood, it can be hard to believe it is any different. However, we can gradually learn we don't have to be as afraid because the things we used to be afraid of are less likely to happen now.

Spiritual Factors

Aggie's lion trainer grew up with parents who taught him about God and that God would always be with him and help him. Learning to be a lion trainer was something he'd always wanted to do, but it was a really scary thing to think about doing. What if the lion hurt him? What if he wasn't good at it, and Aggie got hurt?

Aggie's lion trainer worried about a lot of things. When he talked to his parents about this, they reminded him God is bigger than Aggie and bigger than anything that could happen. His parents reminded him that trusting God didn't mean nothing bad would ever happen, but it did mean he would never be alone and would never have to figure out what to do by himself. The lion trainer thought about this a lot as he learned how to train lions. He reminded himself it was his job to learn to be a good lion trainer, but it was God's job to know what was going to happen in the future.

When it was time for the lion trainer to step into the cage with Aggie, he reminded himself God was bigger than Aggie and would help him know what to do no matter how things went. The lion trainer reminded himself God was standing right beside him while he was training Aggie and would help him figure out what to do if he made mistakes. Knowing he wasn't alone helped the lion trainer feel less afraid and try the scary thing he had always wanted to do.

A lot of the things we want to do in our life feel really scary, and we worry a lot about something bad happening or making mistakes. However, God tells us he will never leave us alone. He doesn't promise us bad things won't happen, but he promises he will be there with us when bad things happen and will help us to figure out how to deal with them. He also promises nothing will happen to us that he doesn't know about and doesn't know how to help us through. When we remember this, we won't feel so alone and afraid as we try new things or when something bad happens. We can talk to God, and he will help calm us and will be with us, guiding us.

☰ *Applying What You Learned*

Helping your child externalize anxiety and not see it as who they are is an important part of helping them learn how to manage the worry and anxiety in their life.

1. What is one thing you can do to help your child see anxiety as something affecting them rather than as who they are?

2. What makes it hard for you to see anxiety as separate from who your child is?

3. How can you remind yourself your child is not the anxiety they are experiencing?

Biology, thought patterns, social environment, and spiritual practices all influence whether children struggle with worry or anxiety. These same components must be integrated into a healthy plan for addressing worry or anxiety. We'll look at how each of these factors contribute to worry and anxiety and how they can be leveraged to effectively treat them.

FOUR

Biology Affects Anxiety

I frequently joked with my kids during their growing-up years that their teeth were their dad's fault. My family historically has good teeth, but my husband was not so lucky, and he passed this on to our children. My teenage daughter and I quipped that her mouth was worth more than my car (and it was). While my children's genetic code caused their teeth to form in ways that left them vulnerable to cavities, the food they ate and the ways they cared for their teeth also played a role. The same concept is true with anxiety.

Biological Factors Contributing to Anxiety

Many biological factors influence whether a child will struggle with anxiety or develop an anxiety disorder—some we understand and some we are just beginning to learn about. As with many illnesses, we can't accurately predict which children will develop an anxiety disorder. However, we do know biological changes occur within the body when a child has one, and these changes often require medical intervention in order to effectively manage the disorder. Just like diabetes is a disorder created by a chemical imbalance within the body, there is a great deal of evidence showing anxiety disorders also occur because of chemical imbalances. Heredity, chemical imbalances, and other medical conditions all contribute to anxiety, and there are steps that can be taken to treat these biological components.

Heredity

Unlike traits like eye color or illnesses like cystic fibrosis, there is no one gene we can clearly link to the development of anxiety disorders. While this is true, it doesn't mean heredity plays no role. Sometimes anxiety disorders develop as a result of what is called *multifactorial inheritance*. Multifactorial inheritance refers to a combination of environmental factors and mutations within multiple genes that seem to cause an illness or disease to develop. Multifactorial inheritance means no one gene has the power to determine whether a child develops an anxiety disorder. Instead, a number of small mutations in different genes create susceptibility to the illness. When children with this susceptibility encounter environmental factors that push on this genetic weakness, the illness develops as a result.

Chemical Imbalances

Regardless of whether heredity is involved in the development of an anxiety disorder, children who develop anxiety disorders appear to have abnormalities within their body's chemical systems. Abnormalities in as many as ten different brain systems may be linked to the development of panic disorders.[1] In particular, scientists have looked at how certain messenger neurotransmitters within the brain and central nervous system affect anxiety. Remember the image of neurotransmitters traveling across the synaptic gap in chapter 1? If, for any reason, there aren't enough of these neurotransmitters, or they are prevented from traveling from one neuron to the next, the result is a mental illness like anxiety or depression.

The neurotransmitters serotonin, norepinephrine, and dopamine appear to be linked to anxiety disorders. All three play essential roles in maintaining a healthy mood. When children struggling with anxiety disorders are given antidepressants, which increase the amount of these neurotransmitters available for the body to use, their symptoms of anxiety can often be effectively managed.[2] Antidepressants are often considered the treatment of choice for anxiety disorders but, like any medication, have side effects and are not effective for every child. Additionally, antidepressants take four to six weeks to begin working and often must be titrated up to an effective dose, which can leave children struggling with anxiety for significant periods of time after they begin treatment.

Another neurotransmitter, gamma-aminobutyric acid (GABA), is involved in controlling the body's response to stress. GABA binds itself to neurons within the nervous system and calms them.[3] Several studies have shown individuals with panic disorder also have lower levels of GABA than control groups without a history of panic disorders.[4] Medications called *benzodiazepines* enhance the effects of GABA because they bind to the same places where GABA would normally bind.[5] While these medications rapidly calm the body and alleviate anxiety, they are addictive and sedating, and their effects typically only last four to six hours.[6]

The fact chemical imbalances can play a role in the development of anxiety disorders means parents should consider talking with their family doctor, as medication may be needed to effectively manage their child's symptoms.

Illness

Chronic illnesses cause huge changes in a child's body and life. Everything about their world is affected by learning to live with a chronic condition. Frequently, symptoms require monitoring to control the illness and make sure it isn't progressing. Additionally, the child can no longer live believing "nothing bad will happen to me" because something bad has happened. Children often become fixated and obsessively worry about what else might go wrong. This is especially problematic for young children, as they often can't accurately assess which fears are realistic. Chronic illnesses also increase stress on the body as it works to continue doing everything necessary despite the illness. This ongoing stress can gradually deplete the body of the neurotransmitters essential in managing depression and anxiety.

Substance Use/Abuse

I suspect many of you arrived at this section and thought, *Why would substance abuse be in a book about children and anxiety?* However, "decades of research in psychiatry have shown anxiety disorders and substance use disorders co-occur at greater rates than would be expected by chance alone."[7] You may still be thinking, *But my child is young*, or *My child knows using drugs or alcohol is wrong.* While these things may be true, research shows by age nine, children are already starting to view alcohol in a more positive way, and by age twelve, 10 percent of children report they have tried alcohol. By fifteen, 50 percent of teens report trying alcohol, and by their senior year, 70 percent of students report trying alcohol.[8] Children with anxiety disorders often develop alcohol use disorders.

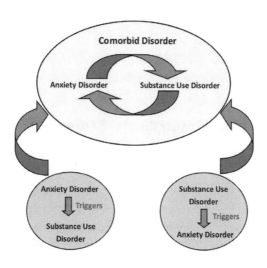

Substance abuse disorders and anxiety disorders are often considered *comorbid* because they coexist, with one feeding into the other. As the figure shows, substance use sometimes triggers the development of an anxiety disorder, although this is not as common as anxiety disorders leading to the development of substance use disorders. About 75 percent of the time, anxiety disorders exist before the substance use disorder develops,[9] and this seems connected to the fact children struggling with anxiety disorders experience incredible distress and often attempt to manage this by self-medicating. For example, a middle school student struggling with anxiety might have a drink to "take the edge off" prior to hanging out with friends, or a high school student might feel that smoking a joint helps them relax and not care if they pass their history test. While these tactics seem effective to the child in the moment, they don't address the underlying anxiety disorder and are particularly problematic for children because their brains are still developing. Additionally, this comorbidity makes successfully treating the anxiety disorder difficult and is also associated with an increased likelihood of anxiety disorders reoccurring after successful treatment.[10] So, while anxiety disorders are only sometimes caused by substance use, it is important to be aware of the comorbidity of these two disorders. Parents need to be aware that children often use substances in an attempt to manage the symptoms of anxiety disorders, and this can create an additional illness that must then be addressed.

Steps to Manage Biological Causes of Anxiety

This list of biological factors is by no means exhaustive. It is imperative for parents to seek medical attention for children experiencing anxiety; a physician can accurately assess the cause of these symptoms and identify strategies to effectively treat them. Because of the stigma attached to mental illnesses, parents are frequently reticent to seek treatment until the illness has progressed to the point their child can no longer function. However, early medical intervention minimizes the impact of the illness and allows the symptoms to be more easily brought under control.

In addition to seeking medical treatment, addressing other aspects of your child's life is essential. Your child's physical health is affected by the food they eat, the stress in their life, the way they think, their sleep patterns, and how physically active they are.

Medication

Just like blood pressure medication regulates a system within the body, medication can be used to regulate the systems of the body that create anxiety. However, unlike blood pressure medication, medications used to treat mental health issues are often misunderstood by parents. Common myths include the following.

"Medication is just a crutch." Truth: the medication is correcting a chemical imbalance within the brain and allowing your child's body to function the way it was created. Medications that treat anxiety disorders do the work your child's body cannot do for itself, giving your child the ability to do the work (like learning to think differently) they *can* do themselves.

"I don't want my child to take pills to feel normal, and I don't want them taking something that changes their personality." Truth: medications used to treat anxiety disorders don't stop your child from feeling what they would normally feel, and they won't change your child's personality. They are designed to manage the anxious feelings, not to stop your child from experiencing life as they normally would.

"Medication might negatively affect their development." Truth: medications approved for the treatment of childhood anxiety disorders go through rigorous tests to ensure they work effectively and won't negatively impact children's growth and development. As you have already learned, a child's brain isn't fully formed, and so the medical professional consulted should be specifically trained to treat both children and mental illnesses. Pediatricians

are specifically trained to effectively treat children but don't always have training in how to treat mental illness. Child psychiatrists are medical doctors specifically trained to treat childhood mental illness. If there isn't a child psychiatrist in your area, be sure to check with your pediatrician or family doctor to ensure they have specialized training in treating childhood mental illness.

"If I allow my child to take medication, they will be stuck on it for life." Truth: most medications used to treat anxiety are taken for a period of time but aren't needed lifelong. A small number of children have a body that doesn't consistently produce enough of the chemicals needed to effectively manage anxiety, and they will need to take medication throughout their life to remain healthy. However, this is not the case for the vast majority of children.

While all human brains are structured the same and work in the same way, each one responds uniquely to medication. It is essential to work closely with a doctor you trust because finding a medication that works effectively for your child requires trying a medication, noting what does and does not work, and making adjustments based upon this information. You will need to communicate regularly with your child's doctor about which symptoms are better and which continue to cause difficulty so the doctor can make adjustments. Treating anxiety with medication often requires trying several different medications to identify one that works well for your child.

Physicians use three major groupings of medication to help treat anxiety: antidepressants, benzodiazepines, and beta blockers.

Antidepressants increase the amount of various neurotransmitters available within the synaptic gap by signaling the brain not to reabsorb them. This allows the brain to function as it was designed. These medications are not habit forming but, since the brain is an incredibly sensitive organ, must be started at low doses and titrated up so the brain can adjust. It often takes four to six weeks for these medications to start to be effective. Once the medication starts to become effective, continue working with your child's physician until a dosage is found that manages the symptoms effectively. It is also important to communicate any side effects your child experiences to your doctor. Once your child's symptoms are managed, your child must stay on the medication for between six and twelve months while their brain replenishes its supply of neurotransmitters. Antidepressants must be started and discontinued slowly to minimize the impact upon your child's body.

Unlike antidepressants, which are not addictive, *benzodiazepines* are highly addictive. They are also highly effective in managing the symptoms of anxiety on a short-term basis. These medications bind to the neurons and calm the neural activity. They have a similar effect on the body as swaddling an infant to help keep the infant calm when they are distressed. Physicians often use these medications in combination with an antidepressant for the first few weeks until the antidepressant has time to become effective. These medications are also used as "rescue medications" taken only when experiencing uncontrollable symptoms of anxiety. A child experiencing a panic attack can take a benzodiazepine to help stop the panic attack. If these medications are taken consistently for several months, they should only be discontinued under the supervision of a physician, because abrupt withdrawal can lead to agitation, irritation, seizures, vomiting, muscle cramps, and sweating.

Beta blockers work to interrupt the body's fight-flight-freeze response by blocking adrenaline and noradrenaline. Adrenaline and noradrenaline are the hormones the body releases to prepare muscles for action when the body perceives danger. By suppressing the release of these hormones, it slows the body's fight-flight-freeze response. These medications are also used to treat high blood pressure, angina, and migraines. While these medications are not habit forming, they do lower blood pressure, so your doctor should monitor your child's blood pressure to be sure it remains within a healthy range.

Caffeine

Drinking caffeine does not cause anxiety disorders but it does heighten anxiety for many children.[11] Caffeine hides out in soda, energy drinks, protein bars, chocolate, hot cocoa, and even some yogurts and ice cream. According to the CDC, 73 percent of children consume caffeine daily.[12] Caffeine is a stimulant that causes the body to release more noradrenaline. Children who are more prone to anxiety appear to be more sensitive to the effects of caffeine.[13] Caffeine also raises children's blood pressure, interferes with their sleep, and impacts their mood.

Caffeine also has a six-hour half-life, which means six hours after your child consumes it, half of the caffeine is still in their system. If you allow your child to consume caffeine, be sure it is at least six hours before bedtime to avoid negatively impacting their sleep. Overall, the American Academy of Pediatrics recommends limiting children's caffeine consumption, and this is especially important for children struggling with anxiety.

Diet

When children aren't feeling well, they are drawn to comfort foods—foods that are high in sugar and fat. While these foods entice children, they may also contribute to higher levels of anxiety and depression.[14] This negative feedback loop seems connected to why children struggling with anxiety and depression also have diets low in fruits and vegetables and high in fats and sugars.[15] Instead of comfort foods, a diet rich in complex carbohydrates, omega fatty acids, and adequate water will more effectively help your child feel less anxious and have the added benefit of positively contributing to your child's overall health.

Zinc and magnesium have both been found to lower anxiety levels.[16] Good sources of zinc include oysters, cashews, beef, and eggs. Leafy green vegetables such as spinach, as well as nuts, whole grains, and legumes, are good sources for magnesium.

Adjusting diet is not a substitute for seeking medical attention when your child is experiencing symptoms of an anxiety disorder. However, there is an increasing amount of research showing a relationship between what children eat and the anxiety they experience. Based upon this, modifying your child's diet *as well as* seeking medical treatment may help effectively manage anxiety.

Exercise

When your child is experiencing anxiety, exercise is usually the last thing on their mind. However, it has been proven to positively impact anxiety disorders in numerous studies.[17] Both high- and low-intensity aerobic exercise have been shown to reduce anxiety—you don't have to force your child to regularly go running to benefit from the effects of exercise. The key appears to be engaging in aerobic exercise that uses large muscle groups for fifteen to thirty minutes at least three times per week. Aerobic exercise is activity that raises your child's heart rate into its target range and holds it there consistently. This gives you a broad range of activities to explore with your child, including walking, swimming, water aerobics, jogging, and cycling. If your child is currently a couch potato or hates physical activity, find ways to start small and build up. You may even consider using some video games that encourage physical activity. Work with your child to pick something they think might be enjoyable and start slowly. You may find your child is more willing to engage in physical activity if you do it with them. Be sure your child has had a physical recently if exercise is not a normal part of their lifestyle.

Applying What You Learned

Reading about all the ways your child's biology may be stacked against them can feel defeating. Many of the things discussed in this chapter are not under your child's control. However, there are still steps you and your child can take to effectively care for their body and minimize the impact of their biology on anxiety.

I often use this story from my life when I talk with children: "When I was much, much, much younger, I needed a car but didn't have enough money to get one. What sort of car do you suppose I wanted? You would be right if you guessed I wanted a car like all of my friends were driving. I wanted a brand-new sporty car to zip around in, and I wanted it to be blue because that's my favorite color. However, I didn't have enough money for a new car. My parents helped me out. My grandmother had a car that needed a new home. It hadn't been driven much so it was in good condition, and my parents gave it to me for *free*. The problem with this car—it was *ugly*! It was a grandma car—big, and a really yucky brown color. It didn't look anything like a car young people drive, and it definitely didn't zip anywhere!

"While it wasn't my ideal car, it was a reliable vehicle and would do all of the things I needed it to do. So, I had to decide—would I accept the car and take good care of it so it would run well for a long time, or would I despise the car because it wasn't what I wanted and refuse to take good care of it? The same is true of our bodies. Just like my parents gave me the gift of a car, God gifts us with bodies (vehicles) that house our spirits while we are here on this earth. We don't get to choose these bodies; they contain flaws created by living in a fallen world, and they may not be what we wish they were in many ways. However, just like I had to choose whether I was going to take care of my ugly, brown granny-mobile, we each face a choice around how we will care for the bodies God gives us. Our choices help determine how smoothly our bodies run and how long they last before they start to experience mechanical issues."

Below is a list of action steps you might consider implementing with your child to help them develop healthy habits around caring for their body. *Don't* attempt to do all these activities at once. Work with your child to identify one they will commit to, and then *consistently* work at this activity for at least twenty-one days before tackling another activity. Effective, lasting change takes time, and new habits take at least twenty-one days to form.

1. If your child hasn't had a complete physical in the last year, schedule an appointment with their physician to have one. Make a list of the symptoms your child is experiencing and discuss them with the physician. If you are hesitant to do this, remember there are illnesses that create or mimic symptoms of anxiety, so it is important to your child's overall health that you give the doctor all possible information so they can provide effective care.

2. Keep a record of your child's caffeine intake for a week. If they are regularly consuming caffeine, consider cutting back or eliminating it from their life (maybe your life as well, since children often find it "unfair" if adults have food they aren't allowed to have). Caffeine has a six-hour half-life, so eliminate caffeine within six hours of bedtime to help with sleep.

3. Keep a record of your child's food intake for a week. Pick one thing you can do to increase their consumption of complex carbohydrates, omega fatty acids, or water. Work to make this one change consistently for at least twenty-one days. When you reach the twenty-one-day mark, keep a record of their food intake for another week, compare it to the first log, and celebrate any progress they made toward eating healthier.

4. With your child, pick a way to increase the amount of exercise in their daily life. Start small! Consider how you can partner with them to help them make this change. I am currently competing in a virtual "race" with my daughter

and nieces. My daughter bikes, I walk, and my nieces run. At other times in my life, I have rewarded myself with something I wanted after consistently exercising for a specific period of time. Pick something motivating for your child. New habits take at least twenty-one days to form, so don't make another increase to what your child is doing for at least twenty-one days.

FIVE

How Children Think and What They Think Affect Anxiety

God is relational—Father, Son, and Holy Spirit existing in a perfect love relationship. Each member of the Trinity loves the others perfectly and receives love from the others perfectly. From this love relationship, God created Adam. God formed Adam and then spoke identity to him by naming him. Adam lived in a perfect relationship with God; he received love and identity from God and, because of this, perfectly loved God.

God then said, "It is not good for the man to be alone" (Gen. 2:18). What God had created didn't replicate what he knew to be perfect love. So God created Eve, and from the perfect love Adam had received from God, Adam spoke identity over Eve by naming her. Thus, a perfect representation of the triune God's love relationship was created on earth. God created humanity to need each other to tell us who we are.

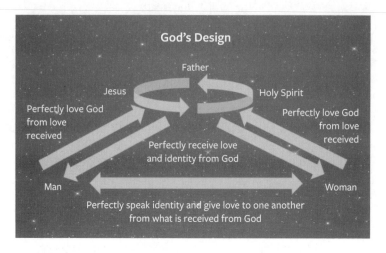

God saw all that he had made, and it was very good (Gen. 1:31).

If only we still lived in this reality! Unfortunately, sin entered the world, and when it did, it brought death—death to our ability to perfectly give and receive love and identity. Children and parents are incapable of perfectly receiving or giving love. Additionally, parents are incapable of perfectly speaking identity over children, and children are incapable of perfectly receiving words of identity spoken over them.

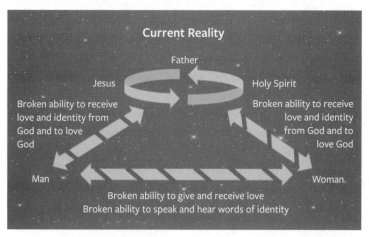

Even though the fall damaged humanity's ability to receive love and words of identity, we continue to need both in order to be healthy individuals. This fundamental need to be in relationships where we receive love and words of identity is why children form attachments.

A child's first attachment is to their mother, and a growing body of research suggests this connection begins in utero.[1] Once a child is born, their primary caregivers become the source for meeting all their physical and emotional needs. From the moment a child is born, they begin interacting with the world around them and creating mental models. A *mental model* is an internal set of assumptions about something that helps children understand new data coming into the brain and predict what may happen in the future based upon past experiences.[2] For example, if a toddler is consistently picked up and comforted when they cry, they develop a mental model of adults as responsive to crying and distressing emotions. Based upon this, the child assumes future moments when they experience distressing emotions will be met by adults who will comfort them. Children develop mental models about who they are and about how they can expect others to respond to them. Parents and other caregivers are the primary source children use when developing these models. While these basic beliefs are affected throughout a child's life, their "bedrock" is formed in the first years of life.[3] This bedrock is formed through a child's experiences and the meaning they give to these experiences. A child's brain encodes and stores this information as memories they later draw upon in new situations.

Before we delve into what children learn and the meaning they give it, let's explore the different types of memories children form and draw upon. Psychologists divide memory into two broad categories:

Implicit memory: skills, procedures, or associations that are automatic and children don't consciously recall.[4]

Examples of this include being fearful of dogs if the child was bitten by one when they were an infant, knowing how to walk, and knowing how to tie their shoes.

Explicit memory: facts and experiences children are consciously aware of and require thought on the child's part.[5] Examples of this include learning multiplication facts, remembering a wonderful Christmas present, and knowing how to make a bed.

With these two main categories of memory in mind, let's look at three types of memories your child is creating. These can be either implicit or explicit.

Factual memory: facts children learn are true, like 2+2=4, the world is round, God is love, and so on.[6]

Procedural memory: stored sequences that allow children to do things. Walking is a pattern of muscle movements that happen in a certain order every time. The same is true of riding a bike, brushing teeth, and almost anything children do repetitively without having to think about doing it.[7]

Episodic or experiential memory: experiences in a child's life that form their understanding of themselves and the world around them.[8] If a child runs into the open arms of their father every night when he gets home from work, and he scoops them up to tell them how amazing they are and how much he missed them all day, this forms an experience of being adored that impacts what the child believes about all fathers as well as what they believe about themselves.

Dividing memory into these three categories is extremely helpful, because once children have learned something, they can only replace it with a stronger memory of the same type. For example, if Johnny learned 2+2=5 instead of 2+2=4, he will have to replace this faulty factual memory by learning the new fact. Johnny would repeat 2+2=4 over and over until this new fact "writes over" and replaces the 2+2=5 fact in his brain.

The same is true of procedural memory. If Samantha learns to pitch a softball using poor form, the coach can't correct this just by having her memorize facts about pitching correctly. Samantha will need to slow down her original throwing pattern and learn a new pattern by throwing correctly until the old sequence of muscle movements is replaced in her brain.

Moving on to experiential memory, if Cory learns that breaking down into tears results in people yelling at him and hitting him while telling him only babies cry, he can't change his experience of "crying is dangerous" by learning new facts. Cory can memorize the fact "crying is a normal and natural healthy expression of emotion," but he will still experience it as dangerous. Changing his understanding of crying requires Cory to have repeated and more powerful experiences of being accepted, comforted, and validated when he cries. Only more powerful experiential memories can overwrite original experiential memories. Think about this for a moment—no matter how many times you tell your child they are lovable, if they have intense experiences of being treated as unlovable, the factual information you tell them will simply sit in their brain. They may be able to tell you they are lovable but will continue to experience themselves as unlovable based upon the mental model constructed as a result of their experiences. Until their experiences involve being well loved, their original experiential memory won't be changed.

It is equally important to remember your child's experiential memories represent exactly that—*their* experiences. For example, my children experienced me as "yelling" at them when I was upset with them. They would tell me to "stop yelling," which I found intensely distressing because I grew up in a family where yelling abounded and knew I was doing nothing of the sort. They experienced my stern and direct commands as yelling, and thus, their experience was that when they did something wrong they were yelled at. It didn't mean I was, in fact, even raising my voice. What children remember are their experiences, not necessarily what happened. Our child's experiences need to be treated as valid, but not as a gospel account of reality. My children and I still joke about when they learned what being yelled at by their mother would really sound like. In a moment of exasperation, I took my children to the basement, made sure all the doors and windows in the house were shut, and yelled nonsense words at the top of my voice for what felt like an eternity. Their eyes became as big as saucers, and from that moment on we all had a common understanding of what yelling was. They had experienced yelling and now were open to exploring new language for what they experienced when I was being direct and stern.

With this as our backdrop, let's explore how our child's mental models of themselves and others impact the types of attachments they form and the amount of anxiety and worry they experience.

Competent, Capable, Dependable

The reactions adults in a child's world have to the child's needs determine how this child views both their self and the world. A child's primary attachments teach them the answers to two important questions:

1. Am I competent and capable?
2. Can I depend on others to meet my needs when I am in distress?

These form the child's pattern for attaching in relationships. The answer to the first question forms their view of self and the answer to the second forms their view of others.

View of Self

If Chris's parents give consistent messages indicating they see her as able to handle age-appropriate tasks, encourage her to take risks and try new things, and validate her successes and frustration at failure, Chris's internal identity will be that she is a competent individual, capable of handling situations, dealing with problems, and managing failure.

View of Others

If Saloni cries out in distress, and her cries go unanswered or unanswered for distressingly long periods of time, Saloni will emotionally shut down to avoid the pain of the unmet need and learn she can't depend upon others to care for her when she is in distress. If Saloni cries out in distress and her parents respond but Saloni's cries create distress within them or overwhelm their skills so they are unable to calm her and care for her needs, Saloni learns her needs are too much for others to care for. Not only is Saloni left with overwhelming distress but she has no one to teach her the skills she needs to regulate her emotions and calm herself when she is upset. Finally, if Saloni cries out in distress and is punished with harsh words or actions, she not only learns she can't depend upon others to meet her needs but also learns others may harm her if she has needs.

Attachment Styles

Based upon how children answer these questions of their competence and others' dependability, researchers and theorists have identified four basic attachment styles.[9] While attachment styles do not cause anxiety, they contribute to why children might experience worry and anxiety. By identifying and working to modify a child's basic understanding of themselves and others so it is healthier, we can help children shift how they function within their attachment styles so they more effectively get their needs met and experience less worry and anxiety.

Looking at your and your child's attachment styles helps you become more aware of what you are implicitly modeling to your child and what your child is learning, enabling you to adjust your parenting to better fit their needs. Read on to gain insight—not to assign blame! No parent is 100 percent consistent in their ability to identify and meet the needs of their child, and children don't need 100 percent consistency. Research has repeatedly shown attempting to parent perfectly does children more harm than good.[10] Trust me; as I write each of these sections, I can identify ways I failed to do each of these things in the lives of my own children. When this happens, we should be honest with ourselves and with God about our shortcomings and then do the work necessary to learn more effective parenting strategies—not beat up on ourselves or resign ourselves to "messing up" our child's life.

Stable Attachment Style

Children with a *stable attachment style* have experiential memories that taught them they are competent and others can generally be relied upon to assist them when they have needs. Developing a stable attachment requires primary caregivers be aware of and appropriately respond to the needs of the children emotionally and physically. Parents who calmly respond in an organized and effective fashion to their children's safety and security needs, hunger, illness, or need for emotional comfort provide experiential memories

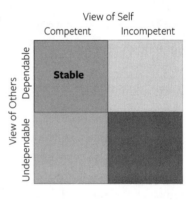

of others as trustworthy and dependable. Over time, these children learn how to self-soothe and regulate emotions from their parents' modeling and can calm themselves routinely without always needing the assistance of others.

Children with stable attachments also have experiential memories of being encouraged to try new things and supported in a calm, reassuring manner as they attempt new things. When these children are unsuccessful, they are comforted, reassured, and encouraged to try again. Little steps toward mastering new tasks are celebrated and reinforced by parents who manage their own emotions, remain calm, and are encouraging throughout the process. Children encode these memories and see themselves as competent and capable of handling new situations, unexpected problems, and disappointments.

Research shows between one-third and one-half of children have a stable attachment style.[11] However, the stablility of this attachment is variable and can change over the course of the child's life. In the diagram below, child 1 and child 3 have a stable attachment but tend to see themselves as less competent than child 2 and child 4. When stressed, child 1 and child 3 might move to a place of seeing themselves as incompetent. Child 1 and child 4 have a stable attachment but experiences that leave them seeing others as less dependable than child 2 and child 3.

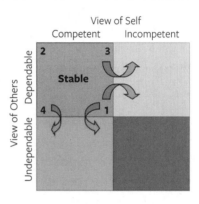

When stressed, child 1 and child 4 may isolate and not share their needs out of fear their needs won't be met in healthy ways.

Having a stable attachment does not preclude children from experiencing anxiety or worry. It does, however, give children a more solid sense of themselves and others from which to deal with anxiety and worry when they arise. For example, if sixteen-year-old Sachi totals the car she is driving in a near-fatal accident, even with a stable attachment she may experience symptoms of acute stress disorder. However, her view of herself as competent to handle difficult emotions and situations will influence how she talks to herself about her experience and the emotional distress she experiences as a result. She is also more likely to know how to calm herself when she finds herself anxiously reliving the events of the accident and will reassure herself that, while this is currently distressing, she won't always feel this way. Sachi's view of others as dependable and capable of responding to her needs will enable her to more easily reach out to others in the midst of her distress, talk about what she is feeling, and ask for assistance. Her internal dialogue and her ability to seek assistance significantly improve her ability to effectively cope with anxiety. Sachi will need people to empathically connect with her and encourage her to see herself as capable of overcoming the obstacles caused by the accident. If adults do this, it will strengthen her understanding of others as dependable and willing to help her navigate life's scary events. A parent's response to a child's adversity can be more important in shaping the child's view of themselves and the world around them than the actual circumstances of the adversity itself.

Children without stable attachments are characterized as having an *insecure attachment style*. Three distinct styles of insecure attachment can be identified, and between one-half and two-thirds of children develop one of them.[12]

Preoccupied Attachment Style

In contrast to children with stable attachments, children with a *preoccupied attachment style* do not view themselves as capable and competent. Their early life experiential memories may have been ones where their parents were not attuned to what they were capable of, so they were given inappropriately difficult tasks that caused them to consistently experience failure. Conversely, the tasks may have been developmentally appropriate but the child's parents were fearful the child would be unsuccesful or experience failure, and therefore overfunctioned for the child or did not encourage the child to take risks and learn from unsuccessful attempts. Such parents are often referred to as "helicopter parents," and their well-intentioned attempts to protect their child from negative experiences actually produce a negative self-concept within the child. Their constant attention and unwillingness to allow the child to experience frustration and failure teach the child the parent is an all-knowing, all-powerful, and dependable adult, and the child needs this individual in order to be okay. They firmly believe others are dependable and competent, but they are incompetent and incapable of managing their own emotions or taking care of themselves.

Children who develop this internal belief system become preoccupied with having someone else in their world at all times and making sure this person is aware of them, taking care of them, and unwilling to leave them. Children with preoccupied attachments have difficulty making their own decisions and are often willing to be in unhealthy, even abusive, relationships just to have someone with them who takes care of them and tells them what to do.

Children with a preoccupied attachment have fewer skills with which to handle anxiety. Their parents don't provide space for them to practice soothing themselves and to develop emotion regulation skills. Children with a preoccupied attachment are intensely fearful of abandonment or upsetting the person they feel dependent upon for their well-being. Just like those with a stable attachment, children with a preoccupied attachment can have a variable sense of their own capability and the dependability of others.

The lack of emotion regulation skills and the fear of losing people they depend on can contribute to chronic worry and to anxiety disorders. For example, if eight-year-old Mateo has a preoccupied attachment style and is struggling with symptoms of separation anxiety, his internal self-talk will likely be about things he won't be able to handle if he goes to his friend's birthday party, his inability to handle his emotions as he thinks about going to the birthday party, and his inability to make sure bad things won't happen if he goes to the party. He will likely struggle with distressing emotions about the birthday party and will tend to overvalue the help others give him while devaluing his own actions. His inability to self-soothe or view himself as someone who can successfully navigate an unfamiliar situation will intensify feelings of being out of control and overwhelmed—all of which feed anxiety and worry. Mateo's parents could encourage him to learn and practice new skills around managing his emotions. They could surround him with dependable people who will be present while encouraging him to do things for himself, celebrating his successes, and refusing to overfunction for him. If his parents do this, over time he will begin to view himself as more capable and be less preoccupied with needing others in order to be okay. This in turn will contribute to a greater ability to manage worry and anxiety in his life.

Avoidant Attachment Style

Up to this point, we have examined attachment styles where the primary caregivers are dependable and adequately meet the needs of the child. What happens if parents are not dependable or don't adequately meet their child's needs the majority of the time? This child may form an *avoidant attachment style*. Imagine being an infant who wakes alone, with a wet diaper, and hungry. You begin to cry out in your distress, and one of three things happens:

- Your cries go unanswered no matter how long and how loud you cry.
- Someone arrives, but this individual feels incompetent and overwhelmed themselves and is unsure what to do to calm you, so they become distressed and break into tears, which creates more anxiety and distress for you.

86

- The individual who arrives is angry you are crying, yells at you, and roughly shoves a bottle into your mouth without ever touching you then stares at the TV in the other room while you eat.

In each of these situations, the caregiver is not attuned to what the child needs and doesn't calmly meet those needs, leaving the child in distress.

Infants whose caregivers are either unable or unavailable to meet their emotional and physical needs will continue to cry until the distress is simply too overwhelming for them. When the distress goes on for too long or becomes too overwhelming, they emotionally shut down

	View of Self	
	Competent	Incompetent
Dependable	**Stable**	**Preoccupied**
Undependable	**Avoidant**	

View of Others (left axis label)

and stop crying because they stop feeling. They learn to take care of themselves by disconnecting from their emotions and from everyone around them. Their experiential memories are of others being undependable and unavailable. These children become self-reliant and find ways to feel better—often by becoming high achievers or by seeking pleasure no matter what the cost. While it would seem as though these children should experience low levels of anxiety because they see themselves as competent, their view of themselves is based upon performance and accomplishment, which makes it about something they do rather than who they are. Their apparent self-confidence is actually a cover that distances them and everyone around them from the deep wounds created when their needs were unmet and others didn't speak words of identity into their lives. For example, infants raised in Romanian orphanages where they were deprived of the ability to form healthy attachments with caregivers had "double the 20 percent rate of anxiety symptoms found in children assigned to quality foster care settings."[13]

God created us to live interconnected lives. Children with avoidant attachments have learned to avoid their awareness of this need by shutting down emotionally and substituting externally pleasurable activities or accomplishments for relationship. This leaves them with a limited ability to encounter and manage emotions and limited skills to ask for and receive the things they need. All of these combine to form an increased susceptibility to anxiety and worry with fewer resources to tap into when experiencing anxiety.

For example, if seven-year-old Adalene has an avoidant attachment style and begins experiencing symptoms of a specific phobia related to dogs after having been bitten when she was four, she will have difficulty letting anyone know she is experiencing distress. Her own internal skills for managing emotion include shutting down or medicating emotions in some fashion. She may work to disconnect from her emotions with an internal mantra like, *You're fine. Don't be a baby. This isn't an issue, so just don't think about it.* If Adalene is able to disconnect from her emotions, she will appear just fine around the dog and may even play with it, but the events that created the panic will remain unprocessed and as powerful as they were the day of the event. She may also stubbornly insist dogs are stupid and only dummies play with them as a way of avoiding her emotions. She will need to continue disconnecting emotionally every time she experiences these symptoms or face a flood of emotions she has limited ability to manage. She will also have difficulty connecting to others who could empathically support her in the midst of her distress and provide reassurance and assistance as she works toward health. She may throw herself into her schoolwork, fill her evenings with watching TV, and self-medicate with as many cookies as she can sneak from the kitchen. None of these activites will address her underlying anxiety, and eventually her unhealthy coping skills will begin to cause additional problems.

For Adalene to move toward health, she will need assistance in learning skills to manage her emotions rather than shutting them down and avoiding them. It will be difficult for the caregivers in her world to recognize her need because she appears capable and self-confident. Regardless of how she appears, Adalene needs experiences of being vulnerable in relationships and having her needs for connection, love, and support validated and appropriately met. Because her experiences in the past told her people are unreliable, this will feel incredibly risky for Adalene. She will need to avoid the trap of simply waiting for people to disappoint her, or inevitably someone will make a mistake and reinforce her belief that others are not trustworthy.

Fearful Attachment Style

Children with a stable, preoccupied, or avoidant attachment style all experience a reliable pattern within their life. Their caregivers were consistently either dependable or undependable, and they were consistently able to see themselves as either competent or incompetent. Children with a *fearful attachment style* have a different experience. In their world, nothing is reliable. Sometimes their caregivers are available and meet their needs, while other times they are either unavailable or punitive. Sometimes they are encouraged to try new things and praised for attempts whether or not they are successful. Other times they are treated as incompetent or punished for not knowing how to do something without first needing to learn and practice. These experiences create a chaotic internal and external environment, leaving the child unsure of what is dependable and what they're capable of.

If you're like me, you read this description and were instantly flooded with memories of your own parenting inconsistencies. However, every parent has bad moments, and this attachment style isn't formed as a result of normal inconsistencies in parenting. Most parents have a predominant parenting style and times when they are inconsistent. Fearful attachment occurs when the swing between good and bad parenting is severe, happens more consistently than any other parenting style, and has no pattern around when it happens, how often it happens, or what provokes the extreme shifts.

Children with a fearful attachment often come from environments with a history of either extreme dysfunction or abuse. Having been unable to determine whether they are competent and whether others are dependable, these children live constantly fearing they will misassess their

capability or others' dependability. These children tend to have black-and-white thinking (beyond what is normal for their developmental age) and swing between extremes. When these children form relationships, people they relate with often feel repeatedly drawn in close and then abruptly pushed away. Children with a fearful attachment often have intense emotional reactions to small experiences of undependability (like a parent being five minutes late picking them up from soccer practice) while simultaneously demanding extravagant expressions from those they form relationships with as proof of their love and devotion.

These children live feeling anxious about every decision they make and are unable to feel comfortable or relax. While this does not necessarily mean they will develop an anxiety disorder, it certainly heightens the possibility and gives them fewer coping skills should one develop. If ten-year-old Vincent has a fearful attachment and is struggling with a panic disorder, he will be overwhelmed with emotions and have limited ability to consistently utilize skills to manage his emotions and calm himself. Some days he may manage well, and other days he will feel helpless to manage his feelings and will demand others do it for him. Simultaneously, he will insist others care for him and rebuff their efforts to help him. Without the skills to consistently regulate his emotions or relationships in which he allows others to consistently care for him in healthy ways, he will remain stuck in crisis, and external attempts to move him out of this will be unsuccessful.

Vincent will have the most difficulty moving toward health because neither his sense of self nor his view of others feels consistent and trustworthy. For him to move toward health, he will need to begin trusting someone enough to risk allowing them to be present with him without demanding they care for him in unhealthy ways or pushing them away and refusing their attempts to provide appropriate care. He will need to trust these individuals enough to learn from them how to strengthen his self-soothing and emotion regulation skills and reliably utilize them. This process will take time and consistent work by him and his caregivers but will result in experiencing less chaos and anxiety.

Your Attachment Style and Your Child's Attachment Style

I suspect many of you identified with at least some of the descriptions contained in this chapter—both for yourself and for your child. If you're like me, you may be convinced you have the worst aspects of all three insecure attachment styles and have permanently damaged your child. Take heart: no one, other than Jesus, has a perfectly stable attachment. This means all parents had times when we didn't experience ourselves as competent or others as dependable to meet our needs. In those places, we developed coping strategies—some of which were unhealthy and left us with characteristics of a preoccupied, avoidant, and fearful attachment. The same is true of our children. No matter how hard we try to parent them well, we are not perfect and neither are they. This leaves them at times unable to receive the love we provide—even when we do it well—and leaves us at times unable to provide the love they need in the way they need it. The key is to be aware of your primary attachment style and the messages it will send your child. Armed with this information, you are better equipped to communicate to your child that you see them as competent and that they can depend upon you to help them when their circumstances are distressing.

To help you identify your primary attachment style, utilize the inventory in appendix A. This inventory is simply a guide to help you identify what might be true in your life. Attachment styles are neither right nor wrong, but understanding them can help you to grow and learn ways of managing emotions and relationships better. This, in turn, will help you communicate the messages you would most want your child to internalize.

Without the assistance of a trained professional, it is impossible to know for sure what your child's attachment style is. However, you can reflect upon their reactions to events and begin to catch glimpses of how they view themselves and the world around them. Thinking in generalities about your child's behavior can help you identify ways to be helpful as a parent. If your child is over age twelve, you may want to have them go through the inventory in appendix A and answer the questions to get an idea of their attachment style. If your child is younger, use the list of characteristics generally true of children with each attachment style below. As you read through the list, circle each quality you believe is characteristic of your child.

Stable Attachment

1. My child makes friends easily.
2. My child appears to enjoy having friends trust and depend upon them.
3. My child finds it easy to become close friends with other children.
4. My child appears to trust others and feel comfortable depending on them.
5. My child doesn't seem to worry about being abandoned.
6. My child is willing to ask for help when they need it.

7. When upset, my child will go to adults in their world for comfort.

8. My child seeks me or another adult when stressed or unsure.

Preoccupied Attachment

1. My child often believes other children do not want to be as close as they would like them to be.

2. My child is often worried friends don't really like them.

3. My child is often worried friends will want to end the friendship.

4. My child prefers their friends don't have other friends or is jealous when their friends have other friendships as well.

5. My child prefers to do everything together with friends, even when friends distance as a result of this.

6. My child is fearful of doing things without the reassurance of an adult that it is the right thing to do.

7. My child asks for help even when they are capable of doing things on their own.

8. My child seeks comfort from adults for even little things.

9. My child becomes stressed or unsure when adults aren't present to reassure them.

Avoidant Attachment

1. My child is uncomfortable if others get "too friendly" or "too close" to them.

2. My child has difficulty trusting friends or others in their world.

3. My child tends to get annoyed when someone tries to get close to them.

4. My child becomes nervous when another child wants to become close friends with them.

5. Friends frequently want to be closer to my child than my child wants them to be.

6. My child seems fine doing things on their own and prefers this over seeking assistance or doing things with an adult's assistance.

7. My child pushes away people trying to provide comfort even when upset.

8. My child seems to shut down emotionally rather than allow themselves to show emotions and acknowledge the need for comfort.

Fearful Attachment

- If you have circled a smattering of answers that are fairly evenly divided between groupings, your child may have a fearful attachment.

These lists may help you to identify how your child is currently attaching to you and others in their world. Being aware of your attachment style and your child's attachment style helps you know what messages you may inadvertently give your child and make adjustments. In the same way, knowing your child's attachment style helps you know what messages your child needs to hear more of and how they may need you to interact with them differently. For example, Scott's awareness of his preoccupied attachment style increases his understanding of how his fears about something happening to his daughter Ashley may inadvertently give Ashley the message she is not competent to handle challenging situations without him. Similarly, Susan's awareness of her daughter Char's avoidant attachment style arms Susan with valuable information about how Char sees the adults in her world. This information allows Susan to focus on consistently identifying and validating Char's emotions so she experiences Susan in a new way. As Susan consistently does this over time, Char's attachment style will likely move closer to being a stable attachment.

While I reference healing as coming through learning skills and having healthy experiences with others, ultimately it is children's experience of God's love and their experience of him speaking identity over them that provide healing. However, children experience wounding in relationships with others—particularly their caregivers—and God pours his love and his words of identity *through* adults in children's lives to bring healing to those wounds. We will talk about how your child's wounds affect their image of God later in this book, along with ways you can create opportunities for your child to experience God's healing love and affirmation.

Applying What You Learned

Below is a list of action steps that may help you adjust your parenting based upon your attachment style and your child's attachment style. Identify one thing you would like to do differently and *consistently* work at this activity for at least twenty-one days before tackling another activity.

1. Given your attachment style, do you need to more consistently communicate to your child that you see them as capable of handling the events in their life or that the adults in their world can be depended upon to be there emotionally and to help them learn to manage their emotions effectively? What is one thing you can do to begin communicating this?

2. Given your child's attachment style, do they need help knowing they are competent to handle the events of their life or that the adults in their world can be depended on to be there emotionally and help them learn to manage their emotions effectively? What is one thing you can do to help them with this?

SIX

Social Environments Affect Anxiety

As a child, every afternoon I climbed aboard a school bus for the bouncy, winding journey to my house. As the trip wore on and my stop neared, I felt my body tense in anticipation. My biggest fear was arriving home to find my parents had moved while I was gone. This fear was so strong that, on the one occasion I remember arriving home to an empty house, I panicked and ran to stop the bus. Amid sobs, I announced to the bus driver I had been abandoned. The kindly bus driver beckoned his frantic charge back onto the bus, drove me to a neighbor's house, and explained the situation. The neighbor took charge of me and watched for my mother's car to make its way down the dusty gravel road. When the family station wagon passed by about five minutes later, I was returned home to a frustrated mother who had been detained and was a few minutes behind the bus with no way to warn me.

To my mother, my fear made absolutely no sense because she had never abandoned me and knew I was old enough and capable enough to manage the few minutes until she returned. I, however, did not see the world through the same lens. At this stage in my life, we had moved at least one time per school year with what seemed to me to be no warning and no reason. Each time, the move would be announced and within a month we had changed homes and changed schools, often with no opportunity to say goodbye to those left behind. For a young firstborn like me whose brain liked routine, predictability, and having a sense of control over her environment, these moves created an underlying, palpable uncertainty around the permanence of anything in my life. This uncertain social environment contributed to an ongoing, low-level worry about who would leave me and whether I could be okay if they did.

As parents, it is often difficult to remember children don't see the world through the same lens as adults and their brains don't function like adult brains. As a therapist, I have to constantly remind myself of this, and as a parent of young children, I often forgot and expected my children to react as an adult would instead of remembering their stage of development.

The environment your child lives in currently and has lived in up to this point contributes to the level of anxiety your child experiences. Environmental stressors also impact whether children develop anxiety disorders. Just like genetics or psychological factors alone cannot be proven to cause anxiety disorders, neither can the stress of a child's social environment. However, considerable research has been conducted around the hypothesis that the more a child's genetics are predisposed toward developing an anxiety disorder, the less stress there needs to be in the child's environment for an anxiety disorder to develop.[1] In the last chapter, we looked at how a child's experiences and their attachment style influence what they believe about themselves and the world around them. In this chapter, we will expand upon this to look at how the environment your child lives in, combined with your child's temperament, influences the level of anxiety they experience.

Every child experiences stress in various forms throughout their growing up years. Stress is easy to identify when we think in terms of large negative experiences like being in a war zone, being the victim of abuse, surviving a natural disaster, or being involved in a major accident. While these are certainly traumatic and stress-ful events that influence those involved, stress encompasses many different types of experiences—both positive and negative. The term *stress*, as it is currently used, was coined by Hans Selye in 1936, who defined it as "the non-specific response of the body to any demand for change."[2] Many different mechanisms exist to categorize stressors, but I have found it helpful to think of stress as coming from five different types of experiences: unmet needs, receiving what is unneeded, onetime events, betrayal, and sustained distress.

Unmet Needs

Your child, like all children, is designed by God with needs. Psychologist Abraham Maslow formed these into his Hierarchy of Needs, which can generally be described as:

1. *Basic care.* Your child's basic needs for food, water, shelter, warmth, and sleep are met.
2. *Safety.* Your child experiences their environment as being one that protects them and feels secure.

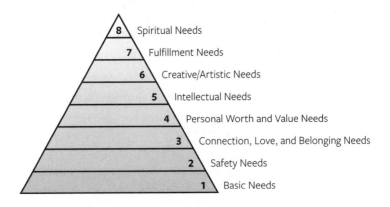

8 Spiritual Needs
7 Fulfillment Needs
6 Creative/Artistic Needs
5 Intellectual Needs
4 Personal Worth and Value Needs
3 Connection, Love, and Belonging Needs
2 Safety Needs
1 Basic Needs

3. *Connection, love, and belonging.* Your child experiences themselves as connected in a healthy way to significant individuals in their life at home, school, and other environments. They can trust these individuals to unconditionally love them, show affection to them, and accept their love and affection when it is extended.

4. *Personal worth and value.* Your child receives consistent messages from others that help them learn to see themselves as a unique and precious individual made in the image of God with worth and value. This in turn helps your child know they can accomplish things, master tasks, and function independently in ways respected by others.

5. *Intellectual needs.* Your child has safe opportunities and encouragement from adults to explore, learn, and understand themselves and the world around them in ways that create meaning and help make their environment feel predictable. This exploration should include affirmation of and growth of gifts and talents.

6. *Creative/artistic needs.* Your child has opportunities to develop and express appreciation for beauty and creativity.

7. *Fulfillment.* Your child has opportunities and resources to successfully pursue personal, professional, and relational desires.

8. *Spiritual needs.* Your child has an age-appropriate pathway to fellowship with God that leads them to see beyond themselves and be motivated to live a life centered around this relationship rather than self-gratification.[3]

If these needs are not met, it creates stress. These needs can be unmet because adults in your child's life refuse to provide what is needed, or they can feel unmet even when all attempts are being made to meet them. Examples of stress produced through unmet needs include things like a parent who spends money needed for food on drugs, a teacher who ridicules a student in class, a coach who consistently overlooks a child, being bullied either online or in person, or a church that teaches "good Christians" couldn't possibly be involved in the art world.

In addition to overt acts that create stress, the same sort of stress is also created when a child lives unsure whether their parent or teacher is going to be upset with them if they don't get an A on every paper, get along with their siblings all of the time, or become the best player on the team. Sometimes a child may experience needs as unmet even when it would appear they are being met; the school bus experience I shared at the beginning of this chapter would be such an example. Needless to say, not a single child has all their needs met at all times. Add to this the fact no child perfectly interprets the messages being sent by the adults in their environment, and it becomes clear every child experiences some level of stress connected to unmet needs.

Receiving What Is Unneeded

Each of the things listed on Maslow's Hierarchy of Needs is necessary if a child is to become and remain healthy. On the other hand, there are many things children do not need, and receiving these can also create stress. American culture is currently filled with the message, "If I could only get to (fill in the blank) then I could be happy." This causes parents to feel the need to fill their child's life with unneeded experiences, things, and people, which creates stress and contributes to worry and anxiety.

The cultural message that parents must provide their child with the best experiences, possessions, and opportunities for that child to become a happy and successful adult is not healthy. Additionally, it makes it difficult for parents to take the steps necessary to teach children how to be content with what they have and who they are. Take a moment to think about this. What would happen if you were able to and chose to give your child everything they asked for, demanded, or thought they needed? As you think about how this would work, you can probably envision the chaos that would ensue and the low probability of your child growing up to be a well-adjusted, healthy adult. My example seems absurd . . . or does it? Many of you live in a culture that invites you to schedule your child's life from the time they wake up until the time they go to bed. You may feel you need to involve your child in activities starting when they are a toddler to make sure you're giving them the "best opportunities." Unfortunately, the result of this is an increase in stress-related illnesses, including anxiety disorders, as well as a decrease in children's actual performance.[4]

According to the International Labour Organization, "Americans work 137 more hours per year than Japanese workers, 260 more hours per year than British workers, and 499 more hours per year than French workers."[5] While parents are working more, children are playing less. Over the past half century, the amount of time children spend engaging in free play (time when they determine what they are going to do rather than being told) has decreased.[6] Recess time at school has shrunk—and sometimes even disappeared—resulting in less opportunity to engage in outdoor free play within a safe environment.[7] Additionally, 85 percent of children also participate in organized activities four or five days per week, and over 55 percent of children go to more than one activity in an evening.[8] When they aren't participating in organized activities, the average child spends 7.5 hours per day utilizing digital media.[9] While free play has trended down and participation in organized activities and digital media use have increased, the levels of childhood anxiety and depression have also increased. One study showed five to eight times as many young people had scores that would indicate they likely met criteria for anxiety or depression than was the case fifty years prior.[10] These are just two examples of how having unneeded things can contribute to higher levels of worry and anxiety.

Onetime Events

If you were over the age of five in 2001, you are likely able to describe where you were when you heard about 9/11. Similarly, if you have been a bride or groom, you can probably describe your wedding experience in great detail. Both are onetime events and, as such, create a high level of stress. Stress is not just connected to negative events. Positive events also create stress, and the body reacts to both. Children can experience intense anxiety connected to being accepted into their college of choice, being chosen to participate in an honor choir, or getting to go to their friend's birthday party.

Onetime events like 9/11, being in an automobile accident, playing at a recital, graduating from high school, going on a first date, or going to school for the first time can produce intense experiences of fear, anxiety, and loss of control. This is compounded for younger children because their brains haven't developed to the point where they know what is truly life-threatening. Yet even for young children, an automobile accident where everyone walks away unhurt will likely produce a different short- and long-term reaction than one where the child or someone they love is seriously injured. Both situations may produce anxiety and even terror when getting into a vehicle for the first time after the accident. However, the more traumatic the event and the less capacity the child has to predict whether this event was life-threatening, the more likely the child is to develop an anxiety disorder that requires treatment.

In addition to the severity of the event, the kind and amount of support the child receives in the wake of the event also affects the level of anxiety they will experience. If Sheila goes through something traumatic and has a community of caring adults who meet her where she is at emotionally, validate her experience, help her understand how dangerous the situation truly was, and support her as she moves through the experience, Sheila will return to her normal level of functioning more quickly than if she perceives she is alone in her experience, her feelings or experience are invalidated, or she perceives herself as required to pretend nothing bad has happened.

Betrayal

Children are born with a deep need to trust. When children trust the people and circumstances around them, it calms their anxiety and allows them to focus on enjoying their life. Betrayal—whether actual or perceived—shatters a child's ability to trust whoever or whatever they perceive to have betrayed them. Betrayal occurs when a child feels harmed by the intentional or unintentional actions or omissions of someone they trust.[11] If your child discovers their friend has shared with another friend something told in confidence, their boyfriend or girlfriend has cheated on them, or their parents lied to them, they will likely experience this as betrayal. In each case, what the child believed to be trustworthy turned out not to be. When this happens, it shakes the child's ability to determine what is trustworthy and creates an underlying distrust of others. This, in turn, produces anxiety, loneliness, and resentment. Since it is impossible for your child to know, with absolute certainty, they can trust others, they must develop the capacity to discern who should be trusted and believe they can successfully navigate the pain involved if their trust is betrayed. If a child is unable to find ways of doing this, they are relegated to a life filled with mistrust and isolation from the things they need to feel safe, secure, and less anxious.

Sustained Distress

Children who are physically, sexually, or emotionally abused live in sustained distress, as do children who live in poverty or environments filled with violence. These examples represent significant and often debilitating sustained duress. However, any environment that is consistently unpredictable or unstructured creates low-level sustained distress.

Another way children experience sustained distress is when their personality and their environment are consistently at odds. I have two children born within eighteen months of one another, and they came into this world with two different personalities. From birth, my daughter was content to be alone and, when she became upset, found it relatively easy to calm herself. However, she was easily distressed by being asked to take risks, deal with unexpected changes, or spend too much time with people. My son entered the world as an emotionally sensitive individual with a high need for the presence of others. In contrast to his sister, he found the chaos created by groups of people to be invigorating and seemed to thrive on risk-taking. As is often the case with individuals who are emotionally sensitive, he tended to personalize the behavior of others and struggled to calm himself when he became upset. Two children with the same parents, living in the same environment, and yet what was distressing to one invigorated the other—how could this be?

Our child's personality is something wired into their genetic makeup *and* something formed as they grow and develop. Personality assessment tools like the Myers-Briggs or the Enneagram have given names to broad categories of personality characteristics in adults and can help parents better understand themselves. However, it is equally important for parents to understand their child's temperament and how it differs from theirs.

As a parent, I repeatedly assumed my daughter would respond to things like I did, which resulted in a mismatch between her temperament and the environments she found herself living in. My earliest memories of my daughter are of her singing made-up songs at the top of her lungs as she danced around the kitchen. This should have cued me in to the fact her personality is different from mine—but it didn't. As I was writing this chapter, I asked her about how she thought the mismatch between her personality and mine caused her to feel anxious as a child. Her response was an immediate laugh, followed by, "Spelling tests." As she said it, I was flooded with memories of evenings spent attempting to get her to memorize spelling words, math facts, and capitals of states. Her answer made total sense!

I am a very logical, sequential individual who memorizes easily and rapidly through rote repetition. It took me years to figure out my daughter heard music in her head all the time, and when she set facts to music, she could easily recall them as needed. It also took me years to learn her mind didn't think logically or sequentially. Living with me created ongoing anxiety for her because she knew my expectations for her and couldn't figure out how to think like me to accomplish those expectations. While she compensated, it wasn't easy, and my inability to understand what made this difficult for her added to her anxiety.

I wish I could tell you I hit the ball out of the park with my son, but I didn't fare much better with him. His genetic loading is more like his father: high energy and highly anxious much of the time. Looking back, many of the things I defined as defiance or willfulness in my son were his emotions overwhelming his skill to manage them. After considerable work, my adult son and I can now poke fun at ways I misdefined his childhood behavior, and he trusts the ways I now more effectively engage him.

I shared these examples of how my personality mismatch with my children created sustained distress for them to help other parents see it is impossible to create an environment perfectly suited for your child. If you are an introvert, you are not going to be able to provide a child who is not as introverted as you are with an environment that perfectly meets their needs. Likewise, if you are an extrovert, you will be unable to provide an environment that perfectly meets an introverted child's needs.

While it might seem personality traits are easily identified and adjusted to, in reality this is difficult and never done perfectly.

However, when we understand each child has a unique tempera-ment, we can make adjustments to meet them where they are. The first step is to recognize each child is a distinct combination of their parents' genetics. Scripture talks about the importance of working with the temperament of our child in verses like "Train up a child in the way he should go: and when he is old, he will not depart from it" (Prov. 22:6 KJV). The phrase "way he should go" refers to the unique way each child is created to function best. Wood-working provides a great example of this process. Woodworkers identify the unique grain of the wood and work with that grain as they create. Wood has more strength going along its grain, and cutting across the grain risks cracking and splintering the wood. Parents can identify the unique "grain" of their child's personality and work with the grain instead of pulling across it in ways that risk splintering or ripping away their personality. When parents actively work to understand the temperament of each child and honor this temperament, it lessens the anxiety the child feels to be different from who they really are.

I frequently see highly distressed children and adults attempt-ing to turn themselves into who they think they "ought" to be so they can be successful, please their parents, or fit in. To lessen their anxiety, they must embrace the way they were constructed by God and learn how to effectively function using their natural strengths.

Mitigating Social Environmental Stressors

If you are like me, you read through the chapter with a rising sense of *But I can't change this or this or that . . . so now what?* While there are many factors in a child's environment parents can't change, there are things parents can do to lessen the impact of stressors and minimize the anxiety they produce. Below are some action steps parents can take to help reduce the stress and anxiety children experience.

Unmet Needs

Read through the list below and identify ways you can continue meeting your child's basic needs and improve in areas where their needs may be unmet.

1. **Routine.** Children need to know generally when things are going to happen, and they need to be able to count on adults to do the things they say they'll do when they say they'll do them. As you look at your child's life right now, do they get up each day knowing there will be a general structure to their day? If not, consider making a schedule. For small children, you can simply do the same sorts of things in the same order each day. For example: we have breakfast, then we brush our teeth, and then we have play time. For older children, you might have a schedule that lists specific things your child does each morning to get ready for school, and they can use this as a checklist to make sure they are ready to go by a certain time each day. For example:

   Before your 7:45 timer goes off to leave for school, you need to:
   - ☐ Get dressed for school
   - ☐ Make your bed
   - ☐ Eat breakfast
   - ☐ Put your dishes in the dishwasher
   - ☐ Brush your teeth
   - ☐ Put your shoes on
   - ☐ Put your coat on
   - ☐ Get your backpack

   Structure this in ways that work best for your family, focusing on the goal of providing your children with a sense of predictability, not rigidity.

107

2. **Sleep.** Children need at least eight hours of sleep per night, with younger children needing more. For anxious children, bedtimes can become a nightmare for everyone living in the house. Parents often become frustrated by a child's refusal to sleep in their own room, go to bed, or go to sleep. Parents often end up exhausted and acquiesce to the demands of their anxious child to get some semblance of a normal night's sleep. Ninety percent of children with anxiety disorders also

have sleep challenges like fear connected to a parent leaving, difficulty falling asleep, difficulty staying asleep, or nightmares.[12] Unfortunately, sleep problems and anxiety problems feed upon each other, with each exacerbating the other, as the drawing indicates.

Sleep hygiene helps children learn how to go to sleep and stay asleep and has three important elements.

a. *Consistency.* Children need to go to sleep and wake within about sixty minutes of the same time each day—weekends, holidays, and summers included. The human body has an internal "regulator" that controls the sleep-wake cycles. When these times vary by more than sixty minutes, the internal clock has to reset itself, and this takes weeks.

b. *Environment.* A child's bedroom needs to be a warm and welcoming environment, free from anything that detracts from going to sleep and staying asleep. You want your child's room to be associated with sleeping.

This means anything not connected to sleep needs to be removed—including toys, gaming systems, cell phone, TV, stereo, computer, iPod, and anything else your child might be prone to play with instead of sleeping. You will also want to avoid bright lights, as they trigger the brain to wake up or stay awake. Nightlights are a compromise and better than sleeping with the lights on, but they can create issues for children that prevent them from doing things like going to sleepovers with friends.

c. *Routine.* A child's bedtime routine starts about an hour prior to lights out by avoiding high-energy, arousing activities. Develop a routine that involves bathing, getting a snack, brushing teeth, and then having some sort of "settling in" activity that doesn't involve screens. The light emitted by these devices activates your child's brain rather than allowing it to settle and get ready for sleep. Bedtime routine should be a pleasant, comforting way of ending the day. Try reading together or talking about the thing you each enjoyed the most about your day. Avoid talking about problems or fears just before bed, as this feeds anxiety. Relaxation exercises can be helpful as part of a bedtime ritual (we will discuss some specific relaxation exercises in chapter 9).

Good sleep hygiene also means avoiding these "anti-sleep" traps:

- daytime naps (for children over age five)
- caffeine (including chocolate) within six hours of bedtime
- liquids within two hours of bedtime
- exercise (or roughhousing) within an hour of bedtime

3. **Unstructured play.** Unstructured play is when children are allowed to play on their own without their play being

directed by adults or other outside sources (coaches, TV, video games, etc.). The American Academy of Pediatrics says unstructured play is necessary because it "allows children to create and explore a world they can master, conquering their fears while practicing adult roles, sometimes in conjunction with other children or adult caregivers."[13] As a rule of thumb, children should have about two hours of unstructured play for every hour of structured play activities in their lives. Parents can increase the amount of unstructured play in their child's life by:

a. *Spending time outdoors.* Create a space outside that is safe for your child and provide toys like frisbees, jump ropes, bikes, balls, or a sandbox.

b. *Choosing true play toys.* My children loved to create forts, doll houses, and a variety of other things out of empty cardboard boxes. Wooden blocks, scraps of lumber with age-appropriate tools, dolls, trucks, LEGOs (without directions for creating something specific), construction paper, colors, and scissors all allow children to engage without telling them what to create. Choose toys that encourage your child to use their imagination and create rather than toys that guide and direct them to do something specific.

c. *Allowing boredom.* Many children will attempt to take the easy way out and get you to tell them what to do by announcing, "I'm bored." When this happens, be prepared to leave their boredom sitting right on their shoulders instead of eliminating it.

4. **Connection, love, and belonging.** Children need to know and experience themselves as valuable parts of a cohesive family. As a parent, you consciously center the things you do around making sure your child is okay and has what

they need to be healthy. However, this doesn't necessarily translate into your child experiencing themselves as loved and belonging. Take time each day to connect with your child, give them your undivided attention, and learn about their world. Family meals facilitate this and have been proven to positively impact your child's emotional well-being.[14] Family meals provide a place for everyone to connect, share about their day, and learn how to have healthy conversations. If your family struggles to find time for family mealtime, try some of the following suggestions:

a. *Choose one meal per week and declare it sacred space on everyone's calendars that cannot be scheduled over.* Choose the meal that gives you the best opportunity to talk without feeling pressured to move to the next activity. When my children were young, this was supper, and as they aged and had more activities, we moved it to breakfast.

b. *If at all possible, gather around a table with healthy food.* If this isn't possible, be creative and try things like picking up food from a drive-thru and eating at a local park's picnic table on the way to your activity.

c. *Ask questions but don't interrogate.* Think about creative questions that engage your child in age-appropriate conversation. You might even create a "random question" jar in case of a lull. Questions like "If I was gifted $100 I had to spend but couldn't spend on myself, I would . . ." can prompt a conversation beyond, "How was school today?" You also want to avoid asking questions with one-word answers like "Fine" or "Yes." Instead of "How was school?" consider "What did you like best about your day at school today?" If they say "Recess," ask what made it the best part. This is also a great time to ask questions about things going on in the world and engage in dialogue around global issues, which helps your children to become critical thinkers. When my children were in early elementary school, we had a lot of conversations around whether they believed there were homeless people living in our town and what they thought would help these people. We also talked about what things they thought would make their school a better place. For older children, engage in political conversations without telling them your opinion or telling them their opinion is wrong. The goal of talking with your children is to help them feel connected and cared for, not to make sure they believe what you believe.

5. **Worth and value.** Your child needs to know they are valued for who they are, not for what they do. Make it a point every day to highlight something you appreciate about them as a person. Instead of saying "I love that you helped me with the dishes without complaining tonight," consider "It was so great to see your ability to think about what others might need and then pitch in! That is a wonderful part of your personality!" The difference may seem subtle, but it matters. By focusing on the quality in your child's personality instead of the behavior, you show you see and appreciate them.

Receiving What Is Unneeded

Read through the list below to help identify ways you can eliminate unneeded things from your child's life.

1. **Screen time.** The American Academy of Pediatrics recommends limiting screen time for children.[15] Excessive screen exposure to TV, tablets, smartphones, computers, and video gaming has been associated with a number of mental,

physical, and social issues for children. While banning all screens from the house is probably not needed or feasible, you can set limits. Consider doing some (or all) of the following:

a. *Set a "screens off" time each day.* At this time, all devices are put on the kitchen counter where they are plugged in to recharge and are not available until the next day. For this to work, this has to apply to *all* screens (including Mom's and Dad's)!

b. *Don't have screens on or present during mealtimes.* Turn the TV off, put phones on the counter, and work to engage in healthy conversation.

c. *Set limits on how much screen time your child can have during the day.* Checkers or marbles work well for this. If your child has four checkers and each can be "cashed in" for fifteen minutes of screen time, this allows the child to choose when they use their time while parents still control how much time they have.

d. *Use screens in common areas of the house.* Placing screens where you will walk by provides a check for children as they are considering what sites to access.

e. *Make sure adolescents know you have the right to check their history and their texts at any time to make sure things remain healthy.* Periodically checking your teen's browsing history and text messages keeps you appraised of the types of conversations they are having and information they are obtaining. Additionally, knowing you can check will help your teen engage their prefrontal cortex and proactively think through the consequences of their choices.

f. *Be aware of what your child is watching and make sure it is appropriate given their developmental stage.* Every TV show, video, and game is teaching your child something. Have conversations with your child to help them think about what is happening and critically evaluate their beliefs around it. With younger children, determine whether or not your child believes what is happening is real or imaginary so you can help them process it.

g. *Consider taking a digital sabbatical.* Find an hour, a day, a week, or even longer when your entire family switches off everything digital and does something together as a family.

2. **Pressure to perform.** It's normal to want your child to do their best and to perform well. However, pressuring your child to perform also has serious negative consequences. Some parents pressure their children to perform well in sports, music, or theater *in addition* to being A students.[16] While you want your child to know you expect them to work hard and do their best, when this turns into pressure to perform children can experience ongoing anxiety that negatively impacts their development, their self-esteem, and even their willingness to cheat. Here are some "tells" to alert you that you may be moving into pressure parenting:

a. *You choose the extracurricular activities your child is involved in.* The younger your child, the more they should be encouraged and allowed to explore a variety of activities without needing to commit to ongoing involvement in any of them.

b. *Your child's performance in competitive sports, dance, theater, or music matters to you.* Children younger than junior high age really don't need to be involved in competitive activities to be successful in these activities when they are older. If you have the choice between a recreational team and a competitive team, choose the recreational team and give your child a chance to explore and learn basic skills while avoiding the pressure to perform.

c. *Grades are more important to you than what your child learns.* Instead of simply looking at your child's grades, make sure you are aware of the effort they are putting in to get those grades and what they are learning in the class.

d. *You try to involve your child in every activity they are interested in or every activity available.* Research shows involving children in too many activities is harmful for their development and emotional well-being.[17] Set limits that allow your child downtime and don't create pressure. At my house, the limit was one extracurricular activity per child at any given time.

e. *You tend to helicopter parent by hovering over your child, attempting to make sure they succeed and don't encounter obstacles or problems.* This inadvertently teaches children they are not competent or capable of managing their lives and need their parents in order to function. If you're reading this and thought, *Phew, that isn't me!* consider the following list prior to letting yourself totally off the hook:

  • You discourage your child from engaging in exploratory behaviors like tree climbing for fear they will be hurt.

  • You consistently are playing with your child and directing their behavior so they aren't alone.

  • You go to extra lengths to ensure your child has a certain teacher, coach, friends, or activities.

  • You monitor their homework and provide assistance until you know they have most (or all) of the answers correct.

- You shield your child from failure by intervening.
- You negotiate your child's conflicts.
- You tell your child's instructors/coaches how to do things differently for your child.
- Your child either doesn't have chores or you do them for your child.

If you made it to the bottom of this list without having to admit you have done any of these things, congratulations. However, for the rest of us, helicopter parenting is an issue! I am the parent of two wonderfully competent adult children and I *still* find myself engaging in some of the things on this list if I'm not really careful. It's easy to do but gives children more advice, guidance, and assistance than they need and doesn't give them opportunities to develop the grit and determination needed to encounter and overcome the normal obstacles of life. If this describes you, consider trying out some of these strategies:

i. Ask questions instead of giving answers. When your child is stuck on a math problem or in a fight with their friend, instead of supplying solutions, ask questions like, "What could you do to try to solve this?"

ii. Before you intervene to do something, ask yourself, *Whose problem/responsibility is this?* If the problem or responsibility belongs to your child, don't touch! Your job isn't to solve the problem or do the task but to help your child learn how to problem solve and cope with the distress caused by obstacles. Think about ways you can help them cope while they problem solve.

iii. Don't do your child's homework . . . not one little piece of it! How your child does on their homework is their responsibility. Teachers get paid to check homework, so let them do their job. If your child did poorly, talk with them about what they learned and what they will need to do differently next time, but don't let them avoid the consequences of poorly completed homework. The caveat I would put around this is if your child comes to you and asks you to read something they wrote and give them feedback. This may be an appropriate ask. Read it and provide feedback around the specific question they asked, and only that question. If they wrote a paragraph that makes no sense, tell them you couldn't understand it but don't tell them how to fix it. If they have grammatical errors, tell them there are errors but don't fix the sentence for them.

iv. Let them solve their problems themselves—even if this means they fail before they get it right. Unless you are planning on moving to college with your child and holding their hand their entire life, they need to learn how to solve their own problems. Learning this will require failing at times, and you get to be the soft-landing spot for them when this happens. Listen well, empathize with how hard it is, and encourage them to look at what they learned, devise a new strategy, and try again.

Onetime Events

As you read through the section on onetime events, if you identified one or more events in your child's past that continue to affect their life, consider engaging in activities to help them to process. When children go through a traumatic event, they need adults in their world who empathize with their emotions and help them make sense of the event. They often don't have language to express what they are feeling and, left on their own, conclude they may have been the cause of the bad thing that happened. If you find an event is having a negative impact on your child or you don't know how to help your child process what has happened in age-appropriate ways, you may want to consider talking to someone who could help you with this.

Betrayal

Parents need to minimize behaviors that could be perceived as betrayal. One way to do this is making sure you don't lie to your child—even to protect them. Children need to be able to trust that the information they get from their parents is accurate. However, they also need access only to age-appropriate information. For example, if you and your spouse are having financial difficulties, and your eight-year-old daughter overhears enough of a conversation to ask, "Are we going to have to sell our house?" don't tell her no if you aren't sure this is accurate. Instead, consider saying something like, "That is not something happening right now or something we want to do. If we ever need to sell the house, we will talk to you about this. You can trust we will talk to you if things are going to change." This doesn't tell your daughter it will never happen but does reassure her it isn't happening right now, adults solve problems like whether or not to sell the house, and adults will give her information when she needs it. When your child experiences betrayal by friends or by other adults, be an empathetic listener who hears and validates their pain and then helps them determine how they want to respond.

Sustained Distress

In addition to making sure we address ongoing stressors within our child's environment, we should also adjust our parenting to fit our child's temperament. Without understanding our child's basic temperament and learning how to create environments for them where they can function effectively, we are fating our child to experience ongoing stress, worry, and anxiety. To help you think about your temperament and your child's temperament, rate yourself and then rate your child in each of the following categories.

After completing this, look back to see where you and your child have similar temperaments and where you are different. Where there are differences, practice reminding yourself your child's temperament is not "wrong" but rather different from yours. Look for ways to celebrate and work with their temperament in this area.

Consider the places your parenting seems to work well and places it isn't. For example, attempting to get my daughter to practice for spelling tests inevitably resulted in a meltdown on her part (and sometimes on mine as well). It also took hours and never produced the desired results. These were all signs my parenting wasn't working effectively. Also, when my son would begin to melt down, I would frequently tell him, "When you're calm again, we can talk about this, and then you will be able to go back out and play." I knew he loved to play, so in my mind this seemed like something that would motivate him to calm himself, have the necessary conversation, and resume his playtime. However, it inevitably resulted in him crying louder and louder for longer and longer. While I need space to get myself under control when I'm emotional, my assumption he needed this as well was erroneous. I now know he didn't have the skill to calm himself when he was upset, so I was asking him to do something he was incapable of.

If I had identified the things I was doing as ineffective, I could have done a bit of research and found other strategies that might have worked better. You can do the same. Look at the places where your parenting doesn't seem to be effective or places on the chart above where your child's temperament is different from yours, and then seek out information around what parenting strategies might work better for your unique child.

Assume children are doing the best they know how to do. Your job is to discover the "grain" God created within your child and then parent them by working with that grain. God created your child, and they are "fearfully and wonderfully made" (Ps. 139:14). As parents, we get to discover the unique temperament and personality God gave our children and grow those strengths so they reflect his character and his love to the world.

1. Activity Level: How much time do you/your child like to spend being quiet versus on the move?

	Seek out and prefer quiet	Prefer quiet to being active	Balance of both	Prefer activity to quiet	On the move most of the time
Parent	O	O	O	O	O
Child	O	O	O	O	O

2. Distractibility: How easily are you/your child distracted when trying to sustain concentration?

	Highly distractible	Easily distracted	Occasionally distracted	Infrequently distracted	Rarely distracted
Parent	O	O	O	O	O
Child	O	O	O	O	O

3. Emotional Intensity: How loud or emotionally intense are your/your child's responses to relatively insignificant events?

	Very intense	Somewhat intense	Fairly balanced	Low intensity	Minimal intensity
Parent	O	O	O	O	O
Child	O	O	O	O	O

4. Routine/Structure: How much do you/your child seek routine in eating, sleeping, and other biological functions?

	Sporadic and unpredictable	Overall unpredictable	Balanced	Highly predictable	Rigid and highly predictable
Parent	O	O	O	O	O
Child	O	O	O	O	O

5. Sensory Input: How sensitive are you/your child to stimulation like sound, taste, touch, or temperature?

	Very sensitive	Somewhat sensitive	Balanced	Limited sensitivity	Not sensitive
Parent	O	O	O	O	O
Child	O	O	O	O	O

6. Approach/Withdrawal: How do you/your child respond to new situations or angers?

	Approach easily	Approach cautiously	Balanced	Withdraw sometimes	Withdraw routinely
Parent	O	O	O	O	O
Child	O	O	O	O	O

7. Adaptability: How easily do you/your child adapt to transitions and changes?

	Struggles significantly with transition or change	Struggles some with transition or change	Balanced	Often adapts well to transition or change	Usually adapts well to transition or change
Parent	O	O	O	O	O
Child	O	O	O	O	O

8. Persistence: How long are you/your child willing to continue an activity when you encounter difficulties?

	Give up easily	Give up fairly easily	Try for a bit and then give up	Persist for quite a while	Persist and have difficulty giving up until you get it
Parent	O	O	O	O	O
Child	O	O	O	O	O

9. Mood: Are you/your child someone who generally sees the world through a positive or negative lens (glass half full or half empty)?

	Glass half empty most times	Glass half empty often	Balanced	Glass half full often	Glass half full most times
Parent	O	O	O	O	O
Child	O	O	O	O	O

☰ Applying What You Learned

Below is a list of action steps that may help you begin limiting the social factors influencing your child's anxiety. Identify one thing you would like to work to do differently and then *consistently* work at this activity for at least twenty-one days before adding another activity.

1. What is one unneeded thing your child receives that could be eliminated from their life? What is one thing you could do to help with this?

2. What is one thing your child is not receiving that they need? What can you do to help with this?

3. How can you work to give your children honest, age-appropriate information?

4. Given the differences between your temperament and your child's temperament, what is one parenting strategy you need to change so you are working with the "grain" of how God created your child? Make a specific plan for how you can begin working to change this.

5. What is one way you can celebrate your child's temperament?

SEVEN

Children's View of God Affects Anxiety

From all outward appearances, I was a model Christian child. I loved going to church and memorizing Bible verses, and I was enthralled with reading the Bible. (To the point I took my Bible to school and read it during free reading time. Trust me—that doesn't make you one of the popular kids!) I knew God loved me and Jesus died for my sins so I could be with God forever. I knew the facts about God and about faith. Yet this wasn't my experience of God. I lived my childhood and the beginning of my adult life feeling I had to be "good enough" to earn God's approval. No matter how hard I tried and how many things I got right, there was always this voice in my head critically pointing out the things I failed to do correctly. I concluded at an early age this was the voice of God letting me know I still hadn't met his expectations.

I wish my experience was an anomaly and most children grow up with a healthy, accurate understanding of who God is and how he feels about them. Unfortunately, this is not the case. No one, not even theologians who spend their lives studying God, has a perfect understanding of him. We are finite beings, and this makes our understanding of any subject limited. God is infinite and we can never fully understand him. However, this doesn't mean children have to live with flawed understandings and experiences of God that create and feed anxiety.

As I discussed in chapter 5, there is a difference between factual memory (2+2=4) and experiential memory (our parents applauding as we hit the T-ball). Children's experiences create a framework through which they understand themselves and the world around them. In this chapter, we will look at how children's understanding of God is formed by their experiences—particularly their experiences interacting with adults.

A child's understanding of who God is and how he feels about them begins forming before they are old enough to use words as their primary form of communication and before they can reason abstractly. Children under age five store memories primarily in the form of pictures filled with emotions. For example, my first conscious memory is of sitting in the backseat of my parents' car, watching my mother cry in the front seat holding my brother while my father angrily drove at high speeds. It is a visceral experience without thoughts connected to it. The memory has no context of its own and is simply an experience of seeing the most powerful people in my life upset, angry, and behaving in ways that made me fearful the car might crash while I sat helpless, alone, and afraid.

When I was an adolescent, this memory gained context when my parents recounted the story of my eighteen-month-old brother drinking out of a pop bottle my father had filled with lawnmower gasoline and then set down on the sidewalk while he finished his repairs. Hearing the story made sense of my memory—intellectually. However, the experience and conclusions I drew as a result occurred long before the context was added and were not necessarily changed after I had context.

The ability to reason in the abstract begins solidifying during adolescence. This means that prior to adolescence, unless children can see it, hear it, touch it, or taste it, they struggle to understand it. God is an abstract concept that children can't experience in concrete, tangible ways. Therefore, they form an understanding of him by looking for concrete experiences to hook to the abstract concept of "God." Sunday school, church, and parents teach children God is powerful and strong. This causes them to link their understanding of God to the strongest and most powerful people in their life and simply assume God is a bigger version of these people. All of this is done without conscious thought and creates a preliminary view of who God is and how he feels about them by the time they are five to seven years old.

By the time children learn to read, they already have a framework for who God is and how he feels about them. They read Scripture through this framework and selectively attend to verses supporting their understanding of who God is. I still own the first Bible I wrote in, and even a casual perusal reveals a plethora of underlined verses about what good Christians should and shouldn't do. The verses referencing his kindness, graciousness, understanding, and care are untouched. As a child I read Scripture through the lens of needing to earn God's approval, and this determined which verses I was drawn to.

Every child has distinct experiences that form their understanding, accurate and inaccurate, of who God is and how he feels about them. Notice I said *experiences*—not reality. As the parent of two grown children, I am consistently amazed at their memories of childhood experiences compared to what I knew I was attempting to provide for them and my own memories of their childhood.

Children need a validating, safe environment where they can articulate their experiences of events and work through the thoughts, feelings, and behaviors connected to these experiences. Your child's experiences do not represent the ultimate truth about what happened and, while you undoubtedly do not parent perfectly, you don't need to blame yourself for your child's experiences and the conclusions they draw about themselves and God as a result of these experiences. One of the best gifts you can give your child is the gift of honesty. Owning when you make a mistake and asking forgiveness is an essential part of parenting and has a profound impact on how children experience our poor parenting moments.

A child's concept of God is originally formed from information that cannot possibly represent God in a 100 percent accurate way, because it is based upon their young brain's interpretation of experiences with human beings. Children's brains constantly take in new information, call up old similar experiences, integrate the new information with the old, and refile the newly transformed information. This process, referred to by psychologists as *reconsolidation*,[1] means a child's image of God is also changed by the things they encounter over time. Thus, even when their original experiences of powerful authority figures are loving and kind, if they later experience a demanding, uncaring, or uninterested authority, this will be added to their original experiences and will alter their image of God. The human brain is remarkably plastic, which means over a lifetime one's understanding of who God is and who they are will be continually growing and changing.

This process happens unconsciously, but you can also deliberately engage in activities with your child to help them develop and maintain a healthy factual and experiential understanding of God. This requires parents to understand how their child's current concept of God is distorted.

Correcting Distortions

I want to reemphasize that distortions of God are based upon a child's *perceived* experiences. No one parents perfectly, and even when parented masterfully, children often experience something entirely different from what parents intend. This is a universal truth within *all* relationships. My children and I have an example we laugh about now—although it wasn't funny at the time! When my children were in elementary school, we lived in an older house with older appliances. One day my son opened the refrigerator, and the contents stored in the refrigerator door plummeted to the kitchen floor as the plastic holding the shelf in place gave way. I arrived in the kitchen to see broken glass, a gallon of spilled milk, and a variety of other condiments seeping across the kitchen floor at varying speeds. I was instantaneously angry—and also aware this was not my son's fault.

I didn't want to spew my anger onto him inappropriately, and I didn't want either of my children to be hurt by the broken glass. As my daughter joined me in the kitchen doorway, I firmly announced, "Go to your bedrooms right now." They both slunk away without comment as I began the task of cleaning up the mess. I sent them to their rooms as a preventative measure—to protect them from me and from broken glass. Little did I know their experience of my actions was that I was so angry with them I couldn't stand having them around, didn't want to talk with them, and was punishing them. I didn't know this was their experience until they were adults! I use it as an example of how even our most valiant attempts at parenting don't always produce the results we want.

The goal of this chapter is to help parents identify ways their child's perceived experiences may be distorting their image of God and implement activities to begin gently correcting this perception. For example, if my child believes God is unpleasable or might abandon them at any time, it creates an underlying fear and anxiety they must constantly work to manage. Correcting distorted understandings of God can help to eliminate underlying worry so my child can live with the calm, secure assurance they are loved by a God who will never leave them, will provide for them, and cares deeply about every part of their life. But how does this change occur?

As I have said several times, factual memory cannot, in and of itself, change experiential memory. However, children do need to know what the facts are before they can know different experiences might be possible. Until there was evidence the world might be round rather than flat, no one would even consider sailing out to see if they would fall off the edge. Once there was evidence the world was round, someone still had to take the risk of experiencing whether or not this fact was true by getting in a boat and sailing past where one would turn back if the world was flat. This same thing is true in relationship with God. While learning what Scripture says is true about God won't change the distortions children have about him, it is a necessary starting point.

I started the chapter with my distorted concept of God as someone who loved me but didn't like me. This remained my core assumption about God until someone in my life heard me say this and asked me what it meant that God loved me. I quoted 1 John 4:8, which says "God is love," to which the individual asked again, "What does this mean?" In the ensuing conversation, we concluded love is defined in 1 Corinthians 13 by a list of adjectives. The conversation ended there, but my mind would not rest. I took each of those adjectives and looked it up in the dictionary, starting with the word *patient*.

> Patient: "Bearing pain or trial calmly or without complaint, manifesting forbearance under provocation or strain, not hasty or impetuous, steadfast despite opposition, difficulty, or adversity, able or willing to bear."[2]

Then I looked up the synonyms for patient:

> calm, forgiving, gentle, quiet, tolerant, long-suffering, understanding, accommodating, easygoing, enduring, even tempered, etc.[3]

Because I was starting to get just a bit uncomfortable about this time, I also looked up the antonyms:

> agitated, loud, rough, troubled, violent, wild, frustrated, impatient, intolerant, unwilling, etc.[4]

128

I was now armed with a fairly complete factual understanding of what it meant for love to be patient. The next part of the process was probably the scariest part for me, but it was necessary to create new experiences that could replace my unhealthy or inaccurate ones. I began to own how I would like to experience God as patient and then asked him to show me how he was patient in those ways. One of the things I wrote was that I would like to feel God wasn't mad at me when I didn't do things right and when I needed to learn before I could do something. Later in the same day, I was reading a book that quoted Colossians 1:22: "You are standing there before [God with] . . . nothing left that he could even chide you for" (TLB). God having nothing to chide me for was inconceivable, and yet there it was in print. As I kept asking God to show me how this was true, he kept pointing out the ways I responded to my children when they made mistakes and were learning new things. I would tell them, "It's okay, let's try again," and in my heart I would experience God saying, *If you are a flawed parent and that's how you respond to your children, why would you believe I would not perfectly do the same thing with you?*

I would like to say this process happened one time and then my distorted concept of God was completely changed. However, nothing could be further from the truth. But over time, my concept of God gradually shifted. I now believe he loves me *and* likes me—even when I mess up. I can't say I do this perfectly, but I can say it is a core belief I live out of the majority of the time.

As this shift occurred, the level of fear and anxiety in my life gradually calmed. I can tell when the old lie is rearing its ugly head because I begin to feel anxious and fearful I am going to make mistakes or lose God's approval.

While the experiences your child needs in order to change their distorted concept of God will vary based upon the age of your child and the distortion they are dealing with, there are some common components that are always present.

1. Identify what the truth is by finding Scriptures that help define it.
2. Allow your child to own how their experiences have not lined up with this truth.
3. Provide your child with a safe and validating environment where they can own their emotions, accurately label their experience, and forgive those they feel hurt them.
4. Work with your child to identify how they would like to experience God differently than they have in the past.
5. Create spaces where your child can spend time with God, allowing him to provide experiences of how he feels and acts toward them.
6. Spend time with your child looking for evidence of God's love and acceptance in their life.

Safe-Place Prayer

Earlier in the chapter, I discussed the fact children need tangible experiences due to their inability to reason in the abstract. God created a wonderful provision for this when he created every human being with an imagination. The human imagination, when used by God, allows him to provide tangible experiences of his presence and interactions with us. These interactions must always be guided by Scripture and never considered to be literal, but they are important for everyone—especially children. One of the ways God can interact with us is by utilizing our imagination during prayer. I first experienced this sort of prayer as an adult but have found children are often much better at allowing their imagination to be one of the tools God utilizes during prayer. The remainder of this chapter will describe a process of utilizing the imagination to allow children (or adults) to experience safety with God and allow him to bring scriptural truths alive to them in meaningful ways.

Safe-place prayer is about allowing God to create a symbolic reality where your child can feel safe in the presence of God. This is a process you will want to do alongside your child, with your child describing what is happening aloud. While God may interact with your child utilizing their imagination, your child may also impose other voices (including their anxious thoughts) onto God. When this happens, you are there to recognize and accurately label what is occurring. In order for safe-place prayer to work effectively, it has to be something your child wants to do—not something you are telling them they need to do. You need to go at the pace your child is able and willing to go and not push them to move beyond what they are ready and willing to do.

Safe-place prayer always starts with you and your child praying and asking God to cleanse their imagination of anything that isn't of him. I often describe this process to children like this: "God created our imaginations like a sandbox or whiteboard where we can be with him and he can create pictures and experiences to help us understand how he feels about us. He gave the whiteboard/sandbox to us and asked us to take care of it. Sometimes we choose to write things on the whiteboard or build things in the sandbox that have absolutely nothing to do with God. If we have a day when we are really mad at our sister about something, we might create pictures on the whiteboard of punching her or we might bury a toy representing our sister in the sandbox to get rid of her. We need to ask God to erase everything on the whiteboard or smooth out the sand so he can use it."

Once your child understands the concept of praying for cleansing, either you or your child can pray and ask God to cleanse their imagination, make it whiter than snow, and use it to bring his truths alive in your child's life.

The next step is to have your child, when they are ready, ask God to create a place in their imagination where they are safe—the safest they have ever felt in the world—so safe absolutely nothing can harm them. Then wait . . . and wait . . . and wait. After three to five minutes, check in with your child to see if they have a sense of anything. If they don't, reassure them this is okay and ask them if they are comfortable continuing to wait. If they aren't, close the prayer and try again another day. For some children, this process will take a long time, as they have difficulty relaxing enough to allow God to create a sense of safety for them. If your child does have a picture, have them describe it to you. You want them to walk around the space, experience it, and describe it in as much detail as they can.

The first time I did this, I described my safe place like this: "A beautiful field filled with lush green grass about six inches tall. The field has a white fence all the way around it made of wood. The fence is about four feet tall and has two rails. The sun is shining brightly, and I can see myself in the middle of the field. I have a white flowing dress on, and I am standing there with my arms outstretched on either side. It is peaceful and warm and although I am alone, I feel wonderfully safe just being me."

Every individual will have a different safe place, and each element of this will be symbolic. For me, the fact my place is out in the open where I can see for miles in every direction and no one else is there is what creates its safety. There are no surprises that can come from anywhere in my safe place. While this represents safety for me, I know other people would feel anything but safe there!

After your child is able to identify their safe place, describe it, and be comfortably present in it, you can gently prompt them forward. When they are ready, they can invite Jesus to join them there and describe what happens. Because every individual's concept of God is distorted, it is important for your child to describe what happens. They may have a scary monster show up or they may have a loving father show up. Either way, hear what your child says, validate it, and then gently redirect any aspects of their description that don't line up with Scripture. If a scary monster who is mad at them shows up, calmly reassure your child that you understand this is scary, have them go back to their safe place, and then talk about how sometimes our own fears or the voice of the enemy tries to convince us God is something other than who he says he is. Verses like "The Lord does not like to punish people or make them sad" (Lam. 3:33 ICB) can be helpful in reassuring your child what they saw is not God, because God can never be any different from how Scripture describes him.

It can be helpful to look up verses about the character of God together if your child is having difficulty being safe in the presence of God. When God passed in front of Moses, he described himself with these words: "I am the Lord. The Lord is a God who shows mercy and is kind. The Lord doesn't become angry quickly. The Lord has great love and faithfulness. The Lord is kind to thousands of people. The Lord forgives people for wrong and sin and turning against him" (Exod. 34:6–7 ICB). Reading verses like these and having your child ask God to create a picture of him that matches can be helpful. It is important that your child's picture of God lines up with Scripture—and that they don't feel they are doing it wrong if their initial picture is different. Pictures that violate Scripture reveal ways your child's image of God is distorted and help you know how to pray for them. Every child will have their own experience of safety in the presence of Jesus, and as long as their picture doesn't violate Scripture in any fashion, all pictures are fine.

This was my experience of inviting Jesus into my safe place: "Jesus is leaning forward with his elbows on the white fence, just watching me and smiling as I twirl around in the grass with my arms out and my dress gently flowing in the breeze. He is a distance away from me on the outside of the fence. Gradually, as I grow more comfortable with his presence, I invite him to come closer. Initially, he crawls over the fence, leans on the inside of the fence, and continues to watch me. Each time I beckon him closer, he moves until on some level he is aware of my discomfort, and then he pauses. He sits on the grass and watches me from wherever he stops."

Over time, I was repeatedly able to invite Jesus to be with me, he joined me as I danced, and eventually I was able to trust him enough to let him lead. All of this took time and involved me learning to trust his calm, smiling presence. I never saw the face of Jesus, yet I knew he was calm and smiling, and I experienced joy in his presence.

Safe-place prayer is one way your child can learn to interact with God and experience his protection and safety in ways that calm anxiety. When you combine it with actively looking at the character of God and having your child ask God to reveal how he's displaying his character in your child's life, over time your child's concept of God will begin to be transformed.

≡ Applying What You Learned

Identifying ways your child's concept of God is distorted and helping them to address this is an extremely important part of managing worry and anxiety. None of us have perfect concepts of God, so this is a process your child will need to engage in throughout their life.

1. Given what you know of your child and their interactions with God, what potential distortions in their image of God do you see? Talk with your child about your observations using age-appropriate language.

2. Talk with your child about the activities discussed in this chapter and make a plan to try out ones they are willing to consider. You can't make your child do anything, so approach this as a team effort!

3. Set aside five to fifteen minutes each day for the next twenty-one days to work on the safe-place prayer with your child.

EIGHT

Partnering with Your Child

Looking at biological, psychological, social, environmental, and spiritual factors is key to developing a holistic understanding of worry and anxiety. Working to address each of these areas lessens the strain on a child's body, mind, and spirit. However, some children have significant stressors in all of these areas of their life and yet are not plagued by worry and anxiety, while others without nearly as many stressors find themselves battling worry and anxiety every day. Counselors, physicians, and researchers have spent years searching for the answer as to why this occurs and are just beginning to develop a rudimentary understanding of possible explanations.

I want to start this section by reiterating that there is no one "cause" and no one "cure" for either worry or anxiety. Both are the result of the complex interaction between all the factors discussed to this point. Having said this, when children who struggle with worry and anxiety are compared with those who face similar circumstances yet don't struggle, a core set of skills begins to emerge as consistently present in those who manage well emotionally. In exploring this further, some of the base tenets around which the fields of psychology and education were oriented have been challenged.

In the seventeenth century, John Locke took ideas from Aristotle and postulated infants came into this world with minds that were a "tabula rasa," which has been translated to mean a blank slate.[1] His belief was that all minds were blank sheets of paper, and it was up to the environment around them to determine what they would become. Additionally, at that time the only mechanism physicians had for understanding the human brain was autopsies. Looking at an inert brain, you get an understandable working theory that all brains are basically the same and function basically the same way with only external experiences changing how they function. This understanding went unchallenged until the invention of the Functional MRI in the 1980s.

The invention of the Functional MRI provided researchers with the ability to see differences in how brains responded to stimuli by measuring changes in blood flow to different areas of the brain in real time. What researchers discovered is that, while the basic structures of the brain look similar, each individual's brain is wired up and responds differently. Within the last decade, as research into this area has expanded, it has become clear some children are born with brains that are extremely responsive to stimuli from the environment and the people around them.[2] Children born with such highly sensitive brains are more attuned to the emotions of those around them and tend to personalize those emotions. They also tend to be more easily impacted and overwhelmed by environmental stimuli. Imagine being an eighteen-month-old boy and having your mother enter the kitchen worried about the presentation she must do at work. Suddenly you are overwhelmed with anxiety—you feel what she is feeling, and you assume she is feeling this about *you*.

Children wired to be more emotionally sensitive experience more intense emotions than other children, which means these emotions frequently overwhelm their skills and leave them feeling out of control. Also, because they are so consumed by their emotional experiences, they are less able to learn skills other children their age are learning. Much of what children learn about managing emotions is discovered by watching those around them, and mimicking what they see in their own lives. Children who are more emotionally sensitive can be so consumed by what they are experiencing they are unaware of what others are doing to cope and don't naturally pick up on the skills their peers are learning. This leaves these children with more intense emotions, less validation from others for what they are feeling, and fewer skills with which to manage these emotions.

Armed with this new information, the field of psychology has begun to recognize the need to teach emotion regulation skills. This recognition caused psychologists to identify and research what skills children and adults need to successfully manage their thoughts, feelings, and behaviors, as well as research how bodies physically react to anxiety. These are skills many children grow up learning simply by being around parents, teachers, and peers. They can also be taught to help manage emotions—including anxiety.

Let me set the stage for why these skills matter by looking at the Israelites. In Exodus, the Israelites have been in captivity for years—through no fault of their own—much like many children are held captive by anxiety. Being held captive meant they could only attend to whatever kept the Egyptians happy and kept themselves alive, much like anxiety makes children fixate on whatever they believe will make the anxiety abate and keep it from reoccurring. God promises to rescue the Israelites and does this by sending a leader, Moses, who has his own anxiety issues (he refused to go when God asked him because he didn't speak well and wasn't sure what he would say). After God miraculously parts the Red Sea for them to walk through on dry land and the Egyptians are killed when they try to follow, the Israelites find themselves in the desert, free from the Egyptians but with no idea of how to live in this freedom. In the same way, many children can't comprehend what it would be like to live without the tyranny of anxiety in their lives.

Having safely delivered them from the Egyptians, God asks the Israelites to wait while Moses goes up the mountain and gets instructions on how to live in this new freedom. They start off okay, but anxiety soon sets in. Mind you, they are fine in the present moment. They have food. They have water. They are in no danger. Their anxiety comes from fretting about what might happen in the future. They start to worry.

If Moses doesn't come back . . .
If God leaves us here . . .
If we are attacked . . .
We need a leader . . .
We need food . . .
We need . . .

This inability to stay in the moment they are currently in, identify the facts that are true of the moment they are in, see themselves as competent to handle the things they have been asked to handle, and trust they are in the hands of a competent God who will take care of them and won't abandon them leads them to seek a way out of their distress—thus they make the golden calf. Their desire to find a way out of their anxiety about what might happen in the future and their fear they have been abandoned by Moses and God lead them to engage in destructive behaviors. Sound like anything you see your child do in response to the worries and fears in their life?

The Israelites later arrive at the Jordan River to cross over into what God promises them will be a "land flowing with milk and honey" (Lev. 20:24), but they don't see themselves as competent and capable, led and empowered by God to enter this new land, conquer those who are inhabiting it, and establish a new life. Instead, they try to figure out if they have what it takes by sending out spies. The spies give them a lot of terrifying data that starts a new litany of "what ifs." They operate out of the fear of what might happen and the assumption they won't have what they need. The result: forty years of wandering in the wilderness.

Fast-forward a bit and the Israelites begin to run low on food. This throws them into a panic. Their response? They begin to blame God and Moses, saying, "If only we had died by the LORD's hand in Egypt! There we sat around pots of meat and ate all the food we wanted, but you have brought us out into this desert to starve this entire assembly to death" (Exod. 16:3). God's answer: manna.

God is actively partnering with the Israelites as the perfect parent. He is teaching them he can be trusted, he will provide, and they can manage their fears as they wait. He doesn't answer their distress by overfunctioning, answering every question they have and providing them with an environment where they have everything they need all of the time. He also doesn't abandon them in their fear. He is clear they are only going to get what they need only for the day they are in. Some of the Israelites are not sure they can trust God and are fearful of not having what they need for tomorrow, so they attempt to make sure they will be taken care of by collecting enough manna for more than one day. The result: the manna rots. God promises he will be with them and will provide what they need for each day, and he is faithful to the promise. When children don't trust their parents or God will be there, or they don't trust that the things they need will be provided, they often jump into the future and attempt to use the resources God has given them for today to solve problems they believe might occur in the future. This doesn't work, creates high levels of anxiety, and frequently spoils the moment they are currently in.

Not long after God provides manna, the Israelites start crying again, and this time they moan, "If only we had meat to eat! Remember all the free fish we ate in Egypt and the cucumbers, watermelons, leeks, onions, and garlic we had? But now we've lost our appetite! Everywhere we look there's nothing but manna!" (Num. 11:4–6 GW). They treat their thoughts and feelings as facts and predict an anxiety-producing worst-case scenario for the future instead of living in the present moment. Their demand for something other than what they have intensifies the mild distress of their current moment.

By the time they arrive back at the Jordan River forty years later, they have learned some different skills and are equipped to trust they will be able, with God's leading and empowerment, to cross over and take the land. They don't have any more physical resources than they had forty years earlier, but having the skills to trust God, manage their emotions and thoughts, and make healthy choices even when afraid allows them to step into the Jordan, believing God will create a way across. Just as the Israelites learned new skills to trust God, children can learn the skills necessary to manage their thoughts, feelings, behaviors, and the physical sensations of anxiety so they can function in a competent manner even when circumstances aren't 100 percent known and risk-free.

The remainder of this book will explore ways you can partner with your child to help them learn to manage their thoughts, feelings, behaviors, and the physical sensations anxiety creates. Prior to jumping into those skills, let's address foundational principles you, as a parent, must consistently embody to effectively partner with your child. First, I want you to notice I used the word *partner*. I chose it deliberately. Your job is to partner with, not to dictate. You can't "make" your child do anything. As much as I would like to believe I can control my children, since the moment they were conceived I have not been able to control their choices or make them do anything. In fact, when they were teenagers, they both looked at me at various times and literally said, "You can't make me," and were entirely right! The first thing we must give up is the notion we can make our child do things differently, think differently, or feel differently. The more we try, the worse things go.

However, you provide valuable input and your presence is important. Effective parenting is crucial for the well-being of children. Children need to feel their parents are partners with them—essential members of the team helping them grow and become everything God intended them to be. Teachers, grandparents, pastors, mentors, coaches, and others are also crucial members of the team, and children need to know each of these adults is there to empower them to become all they were created to be.

As parents, sometimes we play the role of coach—teaching children how to execute the game effectively. Sometimes we are cheerleaders—encouraging children and noticing positive steps they make. Sometimes we are referees—calling a play out of bounds and perhaps imposing penalties. We are also sometimes a teammate they pass the ball to when they're exhausted or boxed in and unable to move. Coaches, cheerleaders, refs, and teammates are important, but none can throw the ball for the player on the field or make the player with the ball do what they want them to do.

God was the first parent and is the only perfect parent. He models for us what it means to partner with children. God doesn't surrender his power, authority, or divinity to partner with us. Instead, he lets us know his heart and his character. Every day, in a million different ways, he reminds us he loves us and we are valuable to him. He is faithful to us even when we are anything but faithful to him. He *is* love, every moment of every day. As we learn to trust him and believe he loves us, he begins to share things he wants us to do and things he wants us to avoid—not to earn his love but to become who he created us to be. Not only does he share with us that he wants us to avoid harboring bitterness, envy, malice, or rage (Eph. 4:31) so they don't kill us but he goes beyond this. He tells us he will be with us (Deut. 31:6) and will give us what we need to do what we can't currently do (Phil. 4:13). When we allow ourselves to lean into his love, trust it, and believe he will be with us in the midst of the muck, our lives begin to change. God models this parenting, and we learn by experiencing his parenting in our life and following his example.

Compare what you learned in chapter 5 concerning how children form foundational beliefs about whether others are dependable and whether they are competent to what I just described about God. First, God shows he is dependable—he will never leave us nor abandon us. Then, and *only* then, he begins to teach us how to function competently as the individuals we were created to be.

Every human needs to feel accepted, heard, and loved by others who will not leave them nor abandon them. Additionally, they need to know these people see them as competent and capable of handling themselves and the circumstances they face. This is especially true of children. No matter how old your child is, if they don't feel accepted, heard, and positively viewed by you, your effectiveness in partnering with them to learn new skills and manage anxiety will be extremely limited. Forming this attachment with your child requires you to manage your emotions, join your child in their world, and allow them to be in charge while you are there.

Managing Parental Emotions

As a freshman in college, my daughter sent me a paper via email to check for grammar. We had done this since she was a sixth grader, but this time she was seven hours away, and we couldn't go through it together with her making corrections as we talked. Instead, I made corrections within the document using a different color font and sent it back to her—never considering she might simply change my red font to black, remove the words I had put a line through, and turn it in. I got the highest grade in the class on that paper—much to my frustration! I like to write, but neither of my children excelled at writing, and I viewed this as an essential skill. I spent hours holding them captive at the kitchen table and going through papers line by line, showing them what needed to be different. I made them correct their papers until they read like I believed they should. Looking back, my fear that they might fail caused overfunctioning. I was picking them up, ball in hand, and running them down the field for the touchdown out of fear they wouldn't run the play correctly on their own. This overfunctioning produced papers written like I would write them, ensured my children got decent grades, and taught them to let me overfunction for them rather than learning the skills necessary to write well. Because I wasn't managing my fear, I taught my children to see themselves as incompetent and to rely upon me instead of risking and learning the skills they needed. It wasn't until my daughter needed to produce work documents without her mother to "proof" them that she had to take ownership of her writing skills and improve them to achieve her goals. If I had managed my fear, she would have had the opportunity to learn this lesson with others her age, instead of as an adult where the stakes were much higher. Additionally, learning as an adolescent would have increased her confidence and sense of independent mastery.

I suspect I'm not the only parent who overfunctions. At its core, overfunctioning is a parent trying to manage their fear and anxiety by attempting to control the choices and behaviors of their child. It teaches a child they need their parent to be okay and can't make good choices without their parent—both of which feed anxiety. My children are in their thirties, and anxiety still washes over me when they describe situations I believe might result in less than optimal outcomes. Fortunately, I have grown some in my ability to manage my emotions and can ask questions to explore their thought processes instead of telling them what to do. I remember to do this by calling to mind the words of a wonderful pastor friend: "Advice offered when unsolicited is actually criticism." When I'm tempted to grab the ball from my children's hands or pick them up and run them down the field, I check out whether they're asking for input. If not, my job is to cheerlead.

Joining Your Child's World

Children's lives center around their parents like the moon revolves around the sun. They are in tune with their parents' emotions and make decisions about what they will and won't do based upon these emotions. All of this makes parents seem larger than life and incredibly competent while children feel dependent and ill-equipped to function separately from their parents. While parents do things with their child, rarely do parents enter their child's world and allow their child to be the coach directing the play. Parents who enter their child's world affirm they are there for them, understand them, and see them as competent.

Child-directed interactions are part of parent-child interaction therapy, a treatment modality shown to effectively increase utilization of anxiety management skills and decrease avoidant behaviors.[3] Child-directed interactions involve you and your child spending time each day with you tuning in to where your child is at and what they are doing. Your job is to enjoy your child and allow them to lead the time together. As your child leads, you cheerlead without directing their activity.

At this point, you may be thinking, *I already do this.* Read on! While this may sound familiar, I suspect you will find it different from what you currently do. When children are allowed to control time with their parents, it builds their confidence and problem-solving skills and can reduce anxiety. Routinely engaging in child-directed interactions also increases the warmth and pleasure in the relationship.

This "special time" doesn't need to be incredibly long but does need to be consistent. I encourage parents to set aside ten to fifteen minutes each day for special time.

Special Time with Children under Twelve

Talk about special time with your child so they understand it is going to happen for a brief period every day. Children are often a bit skeptical about this and may want an explanation. When I was working on this with my children, I explained they were the pros at playing and I wanted to learn from them. You want your child to know you're the learner and want to join their world. If possible, special time should occur at the same time every day so your child can anticipate it and you aren't attempting to cram it between other activities. Invest in a timer so everyone knows when special time is ending. Then work with your child to create a box of things used only for special time. Include things like blocks, crayons, LEGOs, Play-Doh, dolls, farm animals, cars, and other toys your child likes. The key is to pick things that don't have a "right" way to be used (avoid board games, card games, activities with a prescribed set of rules, activities that provoke competition, or activities that produce a winner and loser).

When it is time for special time, everything else stops. Turn your phone and *all* screens off and put them out of sight so you can focus on your child. Let your child pick where you are going to be and join them by getting down on their level. Since asking questions leaves you in charge and the child attempting to figure out the right answer, avoid them. You can start special time with a statement like, "You can pick where you would like us to be for special time today." If they sit on the floor, you sit on the floor too. After they choose your location, use a statement like, "You also get to choose anything you want us to do during special time today, and I'm excited to see what you choose." The goal of special time is for the child to be in control. Use these principles to help accomplish this goal:

1. Children struggling with anxiety need honest, lavish praise. *Honest* is a key word. Never be dishonest, because children will sense this! You want to honestly reflect what you see your child doing and look for the good, creative parts of this to comment on. You may find this requires you to verbalize more than normal. If your child uses multiple

crayons to draw circles on a piece of paper, you might say, "Wow, I'm impressed at how creative you have been by choosing colors that are so different from one another. I'm excited to see what color you pick next." You aren't being dishonest or overinflating your praise by saying, "You are such an amazing artist." Instead, you're accurately describing what you see them doing while also expressing interest in what they will do next. Additionally, make your comments specific. "You're a good kid" is a general statement that is difficult for children to internalize. Praising specific qualities or behaviors helps build a child's sense of what is good about them. "I'm impressed you are being creative by choosing different colors" describes how they are being creative and labels it as a positive attribute.

2. Join your child's play by imitating them. If your daughter lines trucks up on her side of the table, verbalize, "You just put your trucks in a line. I like that, and I'm going to do it too." You don't need to replicate your child exactly, but you should communicate that you saw what they did and are matching their behavior. Imitating them communicates you like their choice enough to replicate it.

3. Be a sports announcer calling the play-by-play of what is happening. If your son begins making a tower of blocks, say, "You're building a tower. Oh, and now you are making it taller by adding more pieces. I wonder what you will do next." This may feel awkward, but practice this skill as it allows your child to know you are engaged with what they're doing.

4. Be enthusiastic but not fake. Spending ten or fifteen minutes with your child can seem like a chore when there's laundry to fold, but you need to enter in and enjoy this time. Your child needs to know they are worth delighting in and evoke delight from you. Be aware of your child's

uniqueness and revel in who they are. Be in the moment with your child and enjoy the moment.

You will need to refrain from some normal parenting activities that will defeat the purpose of special time. Parents should avoid:

1. *Asking questions.* "Do you want to try something else?" and "Do you know what color this is?" may simply be efforts to capitalize on teaching moments but may also subtly attempt to control the play. Instead, reword your questions into statements. For example, "Do you want to use the red blocks?" can become "I love the colors you choose when you build towers and can't wait to see which color you choose next."

2. *Critiquing or correcting what is happening.* It is natural to want to correct your child when they put the cow in the dollhouse bedroom. It's also hard to avoid teaching moments like, "If you hold your crayon like this, it will be easier for you to stay in the lines when you color." Your goal during special time is to empower your child to feel in control and to build warmth between the two of you. Being corrected or told to do things differently doesn't build a sense of competence within your child and doesn't make them feel a warm connection to you.

3. *Taking control.* You may want to make statements like, "Let's put the cars away," and will need to remember to keep allowing your child to lead. Unless they are doing something that endangers someone or something, they get to decide what happens next. Take a step back and allow your child to lead.

Special Time with Preteens and Teens

As children approach the teenage years, they begin acting as though parents are dumb and they want nothing to do with them.

However, parents are still an essential part of a teen's life, and adolescents struggling with anxiety make more significant and lasting gains when parents are involved in their treatment. So, while you can't bring out the tub of toys for ten minutes every day, it remains essential to find regular time together when your teen gets to pick the activity and lead the conversation. Read through the pattern above utilized by parents with younger children and pay particular attention to the elements that encourage warm connection. Teens hate a "twenty question" interrogation, so avoid asking questions and instead work to make statements and reflect on what you see. Additionally, while teens appear indifferent to what you think, hearing words of praise about qualities you see and appreciate in them is invaluable to a teen's fledgling identity.

While essential, it can be hard to build in regular time to connect with your teen amid their hectic schedules. I initiated "date night" with each of my teenage children to create built-in one-on-one time. Date night involved giving my teen a small budget and the choice of what we did. Sometimes we went for ice cream or took the dog for a walk, and on a few occasions my son played Nintendo with me and attempted to teach me how to navigate the game (while finding great joy in mercilessly beating me).

Special time with teens requires parents to comfortably tolerate silence and to listen well. Listen to what your child has to say about their life and the world. If nothing comes up, be okay with this. Sometimes adolescents feel more comfortable talking when they know their parents can't look at them because they are driving. Describing the day's high and low creates a wonderful place to identify with and reflect upon what they share. For example, when my son announced his class discussion that day was "stupid," it provided a place for me to comment, "You tend to be someone who likes to look for different ways to think about things, and I'll bet you were thinking about the topic differently than the class was." Sometimes a comment like this would provide a jumping-off point for the conversation—and other times it didn't. Either way, by offering my undivided attention and reflecting back not only what was said but potential unspoken sentiments, I communicated I was tuned in and available.

———

The components of special time probably seem relatively intuitive and may even be things you believe you are already doing. I would encourage you to diligently work to set aside time and practice these skills for at least a month, even if you believe you already do these things. You may be surprised at how difficult it is to allow your child to lead for ten or fifteen minutes each day as you are fully present with them. The dividends of these ten minutes are worth it! You are investing in your child's belief they are worth paying attention to, they are not alone in this world, and there are things they do well. You are also building a positive attachment with your child that will be essential as the two of you work to learn new skills to manage thoughts, feelings, behaviors, and physical sensations of anxiety.

≡ *Applying What You Learned*

Many of the activities discussed in this chapter will take time to implement effectively. Don't try to do too much at once. It is better to pick one activity and work to consistently do it for at least twenty-one days. The list of questions below may help you identify where you would like to start. Make sure you can consistently do the activities discussed in this chapter before moving on, as the activities in the remainder of the book build on this partnering relationship.

1. What is one thing you can begin doing to build special time with your child each day? Discuss this with your child and craft a plan together.

2. What makes it difficult for you to allow your child to lead without intervening? What is a step you can take to begin addressing this?

3. What is one way you can work to manage your emotions so you can more effectively partner with your child?

NINE

Taming the Body's Anxiety

Once you have established a consistent pattern of managing your own emotions and being present with your child in their world, you can begin to partner with your child to learn specific skills helpful in managing anxiety. The remainder of the book will look at skills your child needs to effectively manage their body, thoughts, feelings, and behaviors. You and your child are going to partner together to tame anxiety, remembering the issue is the anxiety, not your child. To help with this, we will continue to utilize the metaphor of anxiety as a lion needing to be tamed.

"It is God's will that you should be sanctified: that you should avoid sexual immorality; that each of you should learn to control your own body in a way that is holy and honorable" (1 Thess. 4:3–4). These verses are usually used in conversations about learning to manage sexual desires but have a broader application. For all of us, children included, learning to control our body is essential for managing many aspects of life, including our sexuality, and begins in toddlerhood. As parents, we teach our child not to bite or hit, how to hold a spoon to feed themselves, and how to potty in the toilet. We teach these skills deliberately and don't expect our child to automatically know them. However, it is rare for parents to deliberately teach a child how to manage the physical sensations of anxiety.

First Thessalonians says we should *learn* to control our body. God doesn't assume we come knowing how to do this but rather it is something we can learn. Learning involves breaking things down into small parts, practicing those small parts until we master them, and then gradually putting the parts together to form a whole. I grew up playing pipe organ, which provides a wonderful example of this process. Complex organ music has eight to ten notes playing simultaneously. There is simply no way to learn all those notes and the movement between notes all at one time. Instead, for one line of the music I would learn the right hand, then learn the left hand. When I had mastered them both, I would practice both hands together until I could play them both. I would then learn the music for my right foot and add it to the mix. Finally, I would learn the music for my left foot and add it in, so I was now playing all the notes of that first line together. If this sounds slow and tedious, you are right—it was! Learning to control your body is slow, tedious work.

When we partner with our child and invest the time and energy needed to help them learn to control their body, it equips them with the ability to enjoy their life accompanied by a sense of accomplishment and mastery over their life. As parents, this process may feel frustrating, overwhelming, and sometimes pointless. I shared the example of learning to play music to remind you to patiently persist, because the results *will* be worth it. When I work with parents, they often come back to me after the first week of working on skill development and tell me, "We tried it and it didn't work." When I investigate, I usually discover they tried a skill one or two times, and when it didn't "fix" the problem, they abandoned it as ineffective. Over time, I learned to talk about the difference between "trying" and "training." If I *try* to play a new piece of music one or two times, is it highly unlikely I will play the piece without significant mistakes. However, if I practice and *train* myself, I can learn to play a new piece of music proficiently. The same is true of skills—you and your child will need to *train*, and it will take time!

Talking to Children about Training Aggie

Aggie, our lion from chapter 3, operates instinctually. When Aggie feels scared, he roars loudly and paces in his cage. The instinctual part of his brain is finely tuned and hears every little noise and movement around him. Because Aggie lived in the jungle where there were lots of scary things, Aggie's brain learned to alert him to everything that *might* hurt him—even if it is just a leaf falling to the ground. This leaves his body tense and on alert all of the time. Aggie roars loudly, claws at the air, and paces in his cage while the trainer watches. Just like Aggie, when humans experience anxiety it shows up in our body in many ways. For some people it is a tightness in their chest that makes it feel hard to breathe. Other people get stomachaches, feel tinging in their fingers or toes, or just feel tense all over. Just like Aggie's behavior changes, our behavior also changes when we are anxious.

Aggie's trainer will need to help Aggie calm his body before Aggie can learn to do anything else. Learning to train a lion takes a lot of work, and so does learning to manage the anxiety your body feels. The first step is to identify when and how your body is telling you it is anxious. Once you have learned this, you can learn to lower the amount of anxiety your body feels.

Identifying, "How Loud Is Your Lion Roaring?"

Psychologists use a scale called the subjective units of distress (SUD) to tell how intense a client's experience of distress is. You are going to develop a similar scale with your child. Using the image of a lion's roar to describe anxiety, help your child describe what their body feels like when it is totally calm. Next, help them identify the first signs their body gives them when it is starting to become anxious. Many children aren't aware of their body's anxiety until it is high, so it may take some sleuthing to identify the first signs of anxiety. Have them think about things like where their body experiences anxiety first and which parts of their body get tense first. Once they have done this, have them iden-tify what sorts of things tell them their body is experiencing more anxiety. Be sure to stay focused on *physical* sensations. Next, identify what tells them it is starting to get really bad. Last, have them identify what their body feels when the anxiety is at its worst.

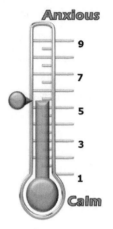

After you've identified the indicators for each level of anxiety, work together to create a scale or thermometer with numbers (or pictures) corresponding to each level. I have created a potential example at the right to give you an idea of how this might look. This scale is going to become a way your child tracks how anxious they are feeling and will provide common language for the two of you around the level of anxiety your child is experiencing.

Using the SUD

Once you have established your SUD scale, it's time to start using it. Start when your child is talking with you about feeling anxious. Ask them to identify on the scale how loud their anxiety is roaring. Don't argue with them about the level they choose—just mark it down. After you have done this a few times, begin to sprinkle in times when your child is obviously relaxed. Again, ask them how loud their anxiety is roaring. It can be difficult for children to identify when their anxiety is calm, so you may need to resist the urge to tell them they are wrong when they identify the level as being higher than it appears to be. Chart their level of anxiety for a week or so and then, together, investigate things your child is doing when their anxiety level is lower. Provide a lot of praise around doing those things and around your child's ability to notice how these activities impact their anxiety.

Learning Lion Training Skills

After you have been able to establish and utilize the SUD for a few weeks, the next step is to begin learning skills to lower your child's SUD. Start by practicing these skills when your child is calm. Only after your child masters them will you begin applying them when your child is feeling anxious.

Breathing

In chapter 2, we looked at what happens when your child's body is stressed and the fight-flight-freeze response kicks in. While things like heart rate cannot be controlled, breathing is something your child can control. Research shows individuals with anxiety disorders take more breaths in a minute, on average, than individuals who don't struggle with anxiety.[1] Helping your child learn to manage their breathing is one way you can help them "short-circuit" the fight-flight-freeze response.

The type of breathing you will learn together is called *diaphragmatic breathing*. It is easiest for children to learn lying down, and then, after they master the basics, begin doing this while sitting up. You will want to round up a stuffed animal and a pinwheel to help them learn the technique.

- Have your child lie comfortably on the floor.
- Lay the stuffed animal on their stomach while you hold the pinwheel below their chin.
- Have your child breathe in through their nose while you count slowly to five at a rate of about one count per second. As they breathe in slowly, they are going to try to

155

expand their stomach so the stuffed animal moves up but the rest of their body doesn't move.

- Now they are going to gently exhale through their mouth while you count to six. Their challenge is to make the pinwheel move for the entire time you are counting. The stuffed animal should also return to its original position.
- Repeat this ten times.

If you find your child is struggling to put this all together, practice just breathing in through their nose and getting the stuffed animal to move. Once they have managed this, add in the pinwheel and breathing out. Don't try to force your child to breathe deeply; remind them they are just naturally breathing in and focusing on getting the stuffed animal to move. Because your child is concentrating on getting the stuffed animal and the pinwheel to move, it will be difficult for them to focus on anything but this exercise, so be sure to limit other stimulation. Once they have mastered this while lying down, practice it in a variety of positions—sitting at a desk (so they can do it at school), taking a slow walk (one count per step), and even going to the bathroom (okay, maybe not for the full ten repetitions). As your child masters slowing their breathing, this will slow their heart rate, which in turn begins to calm their body. By practicing this exercise multiple times each day, it will become second nature for your child, and they will be able to readily access this skill when they feel themselves beginning to become anxious.

Progressive Relaxation

Progressive relaxation was developed by Dr. Edmund Jacobson in the 1920s.[2] He was a physician who began to recognize many of his patients' complaints about aches and pains appeared to be connected to muscle tension they did not seem to know how to release. He developed a series of exercises to help his patients learn how to release that tension. This technique has since been studied extensively in relationship to anxiety and shown to be effective at lowering anxiety levels. Once your child has mastered progressive relaxation, they can use it anywhere and no one has to know they are doing it.

To help younger children learn this process, it can be helpful to play a game I call "Spaghetti and Noodles."

- Start by getting some uncooked spaghetti and talking about how straight it is.

- Then challenge your child to make their arms look like spaghetti. Have them describe what their arms feel like when they are spaghetti.

- Next, talk about what happens when you cook spaghetti—how it becomes really flexible and wiggles around when you shake it. (You may want to cook spaghetti together or have some cooked ahead of time to help small children visualize this concept.)

- Challenge your child to see if they can make their arms like noodles, so when you shake their arm it wiggles around without them doing anything to help. Again, have them describe what it feels like when they have noodle arms.

- Repeat this process of moving from "spaghetti" to "noodles" with their legs, feet, and hands.

- Now, ask them if they can make their shoulders, stomach, face, and buttocks feel the same way their arms and legs feel when they are spaghetti. You can gently lay your hand on the body part they are working on to feel them tighten these muscles and then release them.

- Talk to them about how working to relax their body so it is like noodles can help them feel less anxious.

This exercise, like the breathing exercise, must be practiced so your child can remember how to do it when they are anxious. Also, each time your child practices it, it will lower their anxiety. Doing this even two times a day will lower their anxiety at least slightly. Both exercises work best when you join your child in them. Doing the activities together allows you to model what you want your child to do, lets your child know this is not something childish they shouldn't need to do, and will lower your anxiety too so you are better able to be present and patient with your child.

Combining the SUD, Breathing, and Progressive Relaxation

After practicing the exercises and using the SUD separately for a couple of weeks, the next step is to combine them. Begin by having your child identify when their SUD rises slightly above calm. When this happens, have them use either the breathing or progressive relaxation exercise until their SUD returns to the calm place. You can deliberately practice this by having your child think about something that makes them *slightly* anxious. They should only think about it until they notice their body begin to feel slightly anxious. Once this occurs, they should immediately switch to using the breathing and relaxation exercises until their body returns to calm. Your job, as a parent, is to coach and cheerlead. Coach by counting their breathing for them or gently reminding them which part of their body they are working to relax. Cheerlead by commenting on how hard they are working at this process, how well they are doing as they utilize the exercises, and how much you believe they can learn to do the exercises effectively.

Example

"Now that you have gotten really good at breathing and relaxing your body, we are going to use those skills to help calm Aggie when he roars at you. Can you think of something that makes Aggie roar just a tiny little bit? Okay, Aggie roars when you think about having to do a math facts time-test at school. How about if we think about that now—just until Aggie starts to roar a tiny bit—and then we will see if you can calm Aggie down again. Close your eyes and think about what it is like when you know you are going to have to do a time-test at school. When you hear Aggie start to roar just a tiny bit, let me know and we will stop thinking about time-tests and work to calm Aggie's roar down."

Once your child says they are feeling slightly anxious, transition to the relaxation and breathing exercises by saying, "I'm so proud you have been brave and allowed Aggie to roar just a tiny bit. Now we are going to stop thinking about time-tests and work to help Aggie stop roaring. How about if we start by breathing together. Let's sit facing one another and breathe together. You watch me and I'll watch you. I will count and we are going to breathe in and out five times. While we do this, I want you to remind Aggie he can calm down, and watch for signs he is listening and calming down."

Once you complete the breathing exercise, move to the relaxation exercise and do this together. If, at the end of the relaxation exercise, your child reports Aggie isn't totally calm, start over with the breathing and repeat the process until Aggie has calmed down and they are ready to go play or do something different. Be sure to get back to calm before discontinuing the exercise so your child sees these skills work and understands they can do these exercises and be okay. Leaving your child in an anxious place will make them want to avoid practicing in the future, so be sure you tackle this when you don't have something else planned after the practice session.

Taking It to the Next Level

As your child becomes proficient at returning their body to calm from mildly anxious, the next step is to utilize this same process in situations where they are experiencing more anxiety. Once these two levels have been successfully mastered, it is time to begin talking about how to do this when their body roars "out the top." Talk about the fact they aren't going to feel like using these skills when their body is highly anxious. You may want to use examples from your life of when you had to choose to do something even though you didn't want to because you knew it would help in the long run. You will also want to talk about the fact these skills won't make their body's anxiety disappear right away. Remind them of how long it took to return their body to calm from slightly anxious as a way of helping them remember they will need to use these skills over and over until they feel calm instead of doing them one or two times and then giving up because it didn't fix everything.

Example

"You have gotten really good at using your breathing and relaxation. You are so good at this now that I bet we could begin using these skills when Aggie is *really* roaring. I know this happens at night when you get into bed and Mom and Dad are ready to leave the room. What if we try using these exercises tonight when Aggie roars? If you are willing to do this, I will lay on the floor in your room and practice them with you the first night, and then you can practice them on your own the next night. How does that sound?"

By practicing with them the first night, you help your child to know how to use the skills when they are highly anxious, provide space to reinforce how proud you are that they are being brave, and reinforce how much you believe they can learn to manage high levels of anxiety. You may need to do this several nights prior to having them practice on their own if your child is highly anxious.

Parental Tips

1. The younger your child is, the more you are going to need to be present with them and direct the process. However, don't assume your teenager is going to be able to do this without your guidance and cheerleading! Plan to be present with your child—no matter what their age—and

to participate in the exercises with them until they are comfortable.

2. The more anxious your child is, the less they will be responsive to words. When your child rates their SUD above a seven on a ten-point scale, they are in significant distress. Remember, anxiety is created by the limbic system going into fight-flight-freeze. The limbic system is instinctual and doesn't respond to words. When your child's distress is high, you will want to move toward tactile things that are calming. For young children, scooping them up and rocking them or holding them on your lap may be helpful. For older children, sitting beside them on the couch and gently putting your arm around them or laying your hand on their leg may be helpful. If your child doesn't particularly like to be touched, consider a weighted blanket as an option for them to use when they are feeling high levels of distress. No matter the age of your child, remember you can't talk them out of their anxiety!

☰ Applying What You Learned

Helping children learn skills to calm their physical body is an extremely important part of managing worry and anxiety, but it also takes time and a *lot* of practice.

1. Talk with your child about the activities discussed in this chapter to learn to calm their body and make a plan together for beginning the process of learning these skills. You can't make your child do anything, so approach this as a team effort.

2. As you read the chapter, which aspects seemed like they would be the most difficult for you to implement? What is something you can do to help with these areas?

3. Set aside fifteen to thirty minutes each day for the next twenty-one days to work on the breathing and the progressive relaxation exercises. Make this an activity on the family calendar and don't schedule over it. After you complete these days of practice, spend the next twenty-one days working on practicing these skills when your child is feeling anxious.

TEN

Taming Anxious Belief Systems

As I mentioned in the previous chapter, in elementary school I started taking organ lessons. By the time I was in seventh grade, my teacher wanted me to begin playing for the Sunday morning church service. I was excited at the prospect and set about memorizing the first hymn assigned to me. I spent hours practicing until we were positive I was ready to lead the congregation. She played the prelude and then slid over on the bench. I climbed up beside her, activated the appropriate organ stops, and began to play. Everything went exactly as planned through the first two stanzas. However, as we approached the end of the second phrase, a series of thoughts began flitting through my mind. *What if you mess up? You can't mess up. Everyone's looking, so don't mess up. If you mess up, everyone will know. She's counting on you, and you don't want to let her down. You can't mess up.*

Even as I type these thoughts today, I can feel my body reacting as it did when they first flooded my young mind. Anxiety began to course through my body. I continued to play, but my hands began to shake as my body pumped out adrenaline. The further I went without making a mistake, the more intense the thoughts became and the more my hands began to shake. Eventually, the fear overwhelmed my muscle memory, and I made my first mistake. With the first sour note, my thoughts immediately shifted from *You can't mess up* to *Oh no, you messed up . . . fix it . . . fix it . . . fix it.* This, of course, intensified my fear to the point I totally lost my place in the hymn and the music quickly ground to a halt. It didn't matter that my teacher sat beside me calmly whispering reassuring words, and it didn't matter that the congregation graciously allowed me to falter and restart. The only thoughts in my head were about how I had failed, was a failure, and would never get it right.

I wish I could tell you this happened just once. Though I memorized beautiful toccatas, fugues, and concertos over the year and played each of them hundreds of times without mistakes, during church services I would grind to a halt having made so many mistakes I couldn't recover. My thoughts were my own worst enemy. While I did not and do not have an anxiety disorder, I did have disordered thought patterns that created anxiety for me. Those thought patterns came from an underlying belief system I had developed over the years.

Stated Beliefs

Children learn about themselves and the world around them in two ways: through what they are told by others and through their personal experiences. When things they are told by others either have not been tested or contradict something they personally experience, these beliefs are likely to be things they state are true but don't experience as true.

Children have stated beliefs about many things: what their parents believe is true about them, whether or not they are smart, and the list goes on. In chapter 5 we talked about factual, procedural, and episodic memories. *Stated beliefs* are highly informed by a child's factual memory—the things the child has been taught are facts and are therefore true. For example, my son believed large black dogs were scary and could hurt him until I told him this was not true and he could pet the black dog from the neighborhood. Following this, my son's stated belief changed. He could say in a fairly convincing voice—while sitting in the safety of our living room with no black dogs in sight—that he believed big black dogs were not mean and wouldn't hurt him.

Enacted Beliefs

In addition to stated beliefs, children also have *enacted beliefs*, which are beliefs they act upon. My son had changed his factual understanding and now believed large black dogs wouldn't hurt him. However, he still acted on the belief these dogs were scary, based on his experiential memory of the large black dog having scared him when no one was out in the yard to protect him. To enact his new understanding that large black dogs wouldn't hurt him, my son needed to put his stated belief into practice by venturing into the yard, allowing the neighbor's black dog to lumber up to him, and standing there until his fear calmed and he experienced the black dog as safe and friendly.

Children's enacted beliefs are based upon their interpretation of their experiences and are more emotionally powerful than their stated beliefs. This was certainly true for me, as my mental processes when I began to play in church on Sunday mornings exposed a significant gap between my stated and enacted beliefs about myself.

Mindset

Most children grow up being told they are lovable and are deeply loved by the adults in their world. Children raised within the Christian faith are also taught God is trustworthy and will always take care of them. Children memorize Scriptures proclaiming these facts to be true and have some experiences that verify these statements. However, they may simultaneously have experiences causing them to conclude something different. Regardless of how wonderful their childhood, every child's life experientially consists of wanting to do things they are incapable of, failing to do these things repeatedly, and after repeated failure, sometimes learning to do them proficiently. This process of learning is normal. However, the things children experience while learning form their beliefs about themselves. If three-year-old Luna is learning to button her shirt and her parents repeatedly become frustrated, push her hands out of the way while commenting either verbally or nonverbally, "What in the world is wrong with you?" and proceed to button her shirt for her, Luna learns to experientially believe:

- I am stupid.
- I shouldn't need to practice to learn things.
- If I need practice, there is something wrong with me.
- I can't do things for myself and need others in my life to do things for me.
- The adults in my world may withdraw love and approval if I don't meet their expectations of me.

While Luna may grow up stating she is loved and it is okay to make mistakes, if she has pervasive experiences like the one she had while learning to button her shirt, Luna's enacted beliefs won't match her stated beliefs. Her stated beliefs will be what she wants the world to believe, while her enacted beliefs determine how she interprets life events and what she internally experiences as true. Luna's enacted beliefs form her mindset—the established set of beliefs she holds about herself and the world around her.

A child's mindset determines how they interact in the world, what data they attend to within their world, and what data they exclude. This process, called *selective attention*, causes children (and adults) to exclude data that doesn't support their stated or enacted beliefs while attending to data that lines up with what they already believe about themselves and the world around them. We can see this in my experience of playing organ at church. I believed I was only lovable and acceptable when I was doing things perfectly—or at least better than everyone around me. However, I would never have been able to tell you this. The discrepancy between my stated belief that I was a lovable, good musician and my enacted belief that I was only acceptable when performing perfectly created a great deal of anxiety and caused me to exclude crucial data while attending to other data. I had a teacher sitting beside me reassuring me it was okay and a congregation patiently bearing with me, but none of this registered in my mind. While I desperately wanted my stated belief to be true, I was terrified of making mistakes as I believed this would cause others to withdraw their acceptance.

I had developed what Dr. Carol Dweck refers to as a *fixed mindset*.[1]

Fixed Mindset

Within a fixed mindset, children believe the capability or intelligence they have at the current moment represents their maximum capability. Because they are innately aware of where their current capabilities are lacking but don't believe this is changeable, they compensate by attempting to always appear competent. This preoccupation with making sure others see them as competent causes them to avoid challenges, give up easily when faced with obstacles, believe expending effort to learn and grow won't produce positive results, and ignore or be deeply wounded by constructive criticism that could help them grow.[2] This mindset is particularly problematic when it is adopted by children. The essential childhood process of trying something new, failing to do it successfully, learning from mistakes, and trying again until the skill is mastered is thwarted when a child adopts a fixed mindset.

Fixed Mindset: Anxiety and Worry

Children with a fixed mindset frequently have an enacted belief that they aren't capable of learning new things and are not competent to face the challenges of this world. This set of beliefs creates incredible anxiety. To deal with this anxiety and maintain their façade of competency, they spend their lives attempting to determine what might happen ahead of time so they can have a plan to deal with these things if they happen. These children have an internal dialogue comprised of anxious "what if" questions. When sixteen-year-old Jennifer's boyfriend is fifteen minutes late arriving at her house, her mind goes to, *What if he doesn't want to be with me anymore? What if he's cheating on me? What if he thinks I'm selfish because I wanted him to come over here? What if he breaks up with me, and I spend the rest of my life alone?*

Not only does Jennifer ask all these questions in her head, she attempts to figure out how she would handle each of these situations so she is "prepared" in case it happens. While this can seem like wisdom, it doesn't work any better than hitting your finger repeatedly with a hammer in case you happen to slam it in the door later. Additionally, the younger the child, the less capacity they have to determine what things might reasonably happen and what things are unlikely to happen.

When children become fixated on creating solutions to ways things might go wrong, it leaves them ill-equipped to handle what actually happens. For example, I am a positively awful tennis player with a limited ability to hit the ball with my forehand, no ability to hit the ball with my backhand, and probably a 1 in 30 chance of being able to serve the ball without faulting. My son played on the high school tennis team and frequently wanted me to help him practice. To compensate for my weakness as a player, I attempted to predict where he might hit the ball and get there before he hit the ball in hopes of increasing my success. This, inevitably, left me out of position for where he actually hit the ball. I attempted to predict the "what if" and develop a strategy to deal with it. When reality didn't match my "what if," the energy I expended attempting to create a solution left me ill-prepared to handle what happened.

The same is true when children spend their lives attempting to handle all of the "what ifs" ahead of time. It takes a ton of time and energy to run all the potential scenarios in their head and create solutions. The time they spend creating solutions is time they are distracted from what is happening around them, and the energy they expend depletes their resources for dealing with what actually occurs. All the "what ifs" create an ongoing pattern of worry and can feed anxiety disorders.

Identifying a Fixed Mindset

Some parents read the description of a fixed mindset and feel it perfectly describes their child, while others may be unsure. One fun way to identify fixed mindset traits is for you and your child to take the following quiz together. As you do so, think about what you *live* believing is true—not just what you *think* the right answer is for each question.

1. I was created with a certain level of smartness, and that isn't something I can change.

   a. Agree

   b. Not Sure

   c. Disagree

2. How smart I am can increase or decrease depending on if I spend time using and exercising my mind.

   a. Agree

   b. Not Sure

   c. Disagree

3. I can learn new things, but I can't change how smart I am.

    a. Agree

    b. Not Sure

    c. Disagree

4. If my parents are smart I can be smart, but if my parents aren't smart I won't be smart.

    a. Agree

    b. Not Sure

    c. Disagree

5. Learning new things can change how smart I am.

    a. Agree

    b. Not Sure

    c. Disagree

6. People who are good at something are good at it simply because they were born with more ability.

    a. Agree

    b. Not Sure

    c. Disagree

7. If my life is really hard, I won't be successful.

    a. Agree

    b. Not Sure

    c. Disagree

8. There is a limit to how smart I can become.

    a. Agree

    b. Not Sure

    c. Disagree

9. People who are exceptionally good at something have spent a lot of time practicing that skill even if they also had natural ability.

   a. Agree

   b. Not Sure

   c. Disagree

10. Practice won't change how good I am at something unless I was born with a talent to do that thing.

   a. Agree

   b. Not Sure

   c. Disagree

Once you have answered all ten questions, tally up your points using the key below.

1. A=1; B=2; C=3
2. A=3, B=2; C=1
3. A=1, B=2; C=3
4. A=1; B=2; C=3
5. A=3; B=2; C=1
6. A=1; B=2; C=3
7. A=1; B=2; C=3
8. A=1; B=2; C=3
9. A=3; B=2; C=1
10. A=1; B=2; C=3

The lower your score, the more you operate out of a fixed mindset, and the same is true for your child's score. Regardless of your score, have a conversation with your child around why they answered the questions the way they did. Ask open-ended questions like, "I'm curious about what caused you to say people can't get smarter. Can you tell me more about what makes you believe this is true?" Asking good questions and listening well will help you to identify the experiences causing them to believe their growth potential is limited or that working hard won't really help them to be successful. Pay attention to your score too, as many adults deny having a fixed mindset but the way they live reveals this isn't true. If you honestly answered the questions and revealed a fixed mindset, you can work to change your underlying beliefs—just as your child can.

Is God Trustworthy?

A child's brain thinks in black-and-white absolutes and is ego-centric, making their ability to see things from another's point of view extremely limited. This explains why nine-year-old Jason explodes with "I hate you!" when told by his father he can't have a new toy. Children trust their parents, believe their parents love them, and believe their parents won't abandon them—when their parents are doing things the child wants them to do. They find it difficult or even impossible to believe these same things when their parents are not doing things the child wants them to do, even if the parent is acting in the child's best interest.

A child's ability to trust God is similar. Children see God as trustworthy when he provides them with a safe and secure life filled with the people, things, and experiences they want. Unfortunately, this isn't the life God promised to provide, and when he doesn't, children react to God similarly to when they don't get the toy they want. When children don't get what they have prayed for or believe God should provide, they have difficulty seeing how this can be good and how God is loving.

Children are not alone in this struggle. Scripture is filled with examples of the Israelites concluding God was not trustworthy or good because things did not go the way they wanted—in fact, the Jews had Jesus crucified because he didn't overthrow the Roman government and establish himself as king.

God parted the Red Sea so the Israelites could walk across on dry land and then killed all the Egyptians chasing them (Exod. 14:21–28). The Israelites respond by singing, "The LORD is my strength and my defense; he has become my salvation. . . . In your unfailing love you will lead the people you have redeemed. In your strength you will guide them to your holy dwelling" (Exod. 15:2, 13). A mere three days later, when they can't find water to drink, they complain it would have been better if God had left them in slavery in Egypt. They saw God control water by parting the Red Sea and yet didn't believe he would continue to provide for them because it wasn't happening in their time frame and the way they wanted it to. He didn't give the Israelites a detailed plan for how they would get to the promised land, he didn't tell the Jews how he would establish his kingdom here on earth, and he doesn't tell his children today how he will get them through the hardships they face.

Just like children selectively attend to data that supports their enacted beliefs and mindset about themselves, they also selectively attend to data that supports their enacted beliefs and fears about God. This leaves children with a stated belief that God is trustworthy and Scripture verses memorized to back this up. Meanwhile, they live out of the enacted belief their lives should look a certain way, and since God can't be trusted to do what they believe he should, he can't be trusted to take care of them.

Results of Enacted Beliefs

Children who develop a negative view of themselves or conclude God is not trustworthy end up in a precarious situation. Human beings were created to live interdependent lives, intimately connected to God and others. If a child lives fearful of being discovered as a fraud who is unlovable or less competent than the children around them, they distance from others and project an image of competence while internally feeling deeply afraid and incompetent. A child's fear that God won't meet their needs or won't do so in the way he "should" causes them to attempt to be self-reliant, to predict all of the things that might go wrong, and to ensure they have a plan and the resources to deal with all possible outcomes at all times. Talk about anxiety producing! Fortunately, children's brains are constantly growing and developing, and they don't have to stay in this place. If the adults in their world are willing to help them challenge their fixed mindset and enacted beliefs, they can begin to operate from a growth mindset and can learn to rely upon God to be with them and provide what they need—even if he doesn't provide everything they want.

Growth Mindset

Unlike a fixed mindset, a *growth mindset* starts from the assumption that capability, knowledge, and intellectual understanding grow and develop over time.[3] When children with a growth mindset fail at something, it becomes a chance to learn from their mistake and seize the opportunity to take on a new challenge. They experience setbacks as spaces to problem solve and obstacles as opportunities to strengthen their ability to persevere. Growth-minded children persevere because they see putting forth effort and needing to learn as a natural and normal part of life. These children seek out constructive criticism and view finding ways to master something they haven't yet been able to do as a healthy part of life. They believe they will encounter difficulties and, when they do, will figure out how to use the resources at their disposal to appropriately deal with them.

Going back to my earlier tennis illustration, professional tennis players position themselves in the middle of the court, ready to move wherever the ball is hit. They don't start to move until the ball is hit. Sometimes they choose to move and return the ball, and sometimes they don't move because they believe the ball is going to be out of bounds or impossible to get to. They know the resources they have available and draw upon these resources to play each shot to the best of their ability. They aren't rehearsing what they "should" have done on the last shot while playing the current shot. They also aren't standing on the baseline contemplating and attempting to prepare for all of the "what if" scenarios. Their attention is focused on the present moment, and they see themselves as equipped to deal with whatever comes across the net. Professional tennis players also have coaches—individuals they rely upon to give them advice and help them to become better players. If they struggle when their opponent hits drop shots, they spend time identifying what isn't working and honing the skills necessary to become proficient. Instead of seeing themselves as a failure when they can't do it perfectly, they constantly identify areas where they can grow and work for hours on end to become better. In their world, competency means accurately assessing their strengths and weaknesses as a player, practicing to grow their skills, and entering each game prepared to deal with each shot as it comes across the net.

Children with a growth mindset approach life with this same attitude. They are aware of their strengths and weaknesses, see each day as an opportunity to learn and grow their skills, and approach life as a series of problem-solving opportunities. Instead of running "what if" scenarios and attempting to have a solution to all potential problems, they see themselves as equipped with a set of talents and skills, the ability to creatively problem solve, and a network of caring adults who will help them solve problems or overcome obstacles they encounter. If sixteen-year-old Jennifer is operating from a growth mindset when her boyfriend is late arriving at her house, she may still feel a bit anxious but won't begin running down a list of all the things that could possibly be wrong. Instead, viewing herself as competent to handle whatever happens, she would make a plan for how long she is willing to wait and what she is going to do if her boyfriend hasn't arrived within that time frame. If it turns out something bad has happened, having stayed in the present moment and viewed herself as competent, with the help of God and others, to handle whatever happens will position her with the emotional and mental energy necessary to deal with the situation as effectively as possible.

Parenting toward a Growth Mindset

Children are born with a growth mindset, and this is particularly evident in toddlers. Toddlers see life as an exploration. They are focused on the process of drawing a picture rather than the result. They will obsessively keep trying until they accomplish things they have never been able to do before—like walking, talking, and getting themselves dressed. Unfortunately, many of these children begin developing a fixed mindset by the time they enter school. They begin to compare themselves to others and label themselves based upon how their perceived skills and abilities compare to others'. While parents can't totally prevent this, there are parenting strategies that help children maintain or develop a growth mindset.

Praise effort. It is easy to focus on outcomes, like, "You did an amazing job on the spelling test." This type of statement has two flaws: it may not be true, and it doesn't teach the child to associate effort with outcome. Getting 100 percent on a spelling test may mean they learned absolutely nothing because they already knew how to spell those words. The outcome of 100 percent only matters if it represents learning. Additionally, when we focus on the outcome alone, we don't teach children hard work is valuable and normal. Instead of focusing on outcomes, watch for effort and praise it. Statements like, "I am so impressed you brought me your list and studied for your spelling test last night," teach your child their effort matters.

Reward persistence. Persistence is a skill and, like any skill, must be practiced to become well developed. Watch for moments when your child uses their persistence and reinforce it with statements like, "I know you are really struggling to figure out how to build a three-story building with your LEGOs. I love the way you keep stretching your brain to think about different ways to make it work, and I'm excited to see how you solve this problem."

Emphasize "yet." When you hear your child making statements like, "I can't run three miles," help them to reframe this as a process by using the word *yet*. You might respond with a statement like, "You are right, you can't run three miles yet. I have seen you learn to do lots of things you couldn't do at first, and I'm betting you will be able to run three miles soon if you keep working hard at track practice." Using the word *yet* helps children see learning and growth as a process and see themselves as capable of engaging in this process.

Make mistakes and failure acceptable. Create an environment where perfection isn't preferred. Children need to know making mistakes won't result in being looked down upon, ridiculed, or loved less. When they make a mistake, focus on what they can learn from it and what they plan to do differently next time. Set them up with the expectation they are going to need to practice new things to learn how to do them, and you are okay with this. If your child tries hard and doesn't do well, focus on their effort and what they did learn rather than on the outcome.

These strategies will help your child develop a growth mindset. If you weren't raised in a family where this type of parenting was practiced, you will need to consistently work to effectively parent from this perspective. There are books that can be helpful for you and your child; a good place to begin is the list of growth mindset books for children, adolescents, and adults in appendix B.

God's Ways Are Not Our Ways

God does not always do what children (or adults) want him to do, when they want him to do it, and how they want him to do it. However, this doesn't mean he isn't trustworthy. When I crawled down from the organ bench after what I deemed to be a fiasco, I found myself angry with God for not rescuing me from a situation he was capable of preventing. As I sat in my anger and rehearsed all the ways God could have changed this situation, a subtle change began to occur. I moved from only being angry with God to being angry with God *and* questioning his character. While this might seem like a subtle shift, it is a shift with catastrophic consequences. God is infinite, so he sees and knows things we can't. It is much like a child's relationship to a parent, and we can use this relationship to help children understand God is trustworthy even when he doesn't do things the way children want him to.

Children have numerous experiences where they learn to trust the character of their parents even when they don't understand why parents let something happen. For example, I dutifully took my young children to get their immunizations—an experience I personally hated! Following the nurse's instructions, I firmly pinned my screaming eighteen-month-old son to the table as the needle was jabbed into his leg. From my son's vantage point, his mother—the woman who was supposed to love and protect him from everything bad in the world—was holding him down and allowing something awful to happen to him. No explanation I could give him would ever make sense to him, and I didn't expect it to. I knew this momentary pain would prevent horrible and awful things from happening that he might not survive, but he would never be able to see this and would, hopefully, never experience that greater pain because I was allowing him to experience this momentary pain. I was fine with him screaming and being upset about what was happening. The key: he had to be willing to allow me to scoop him up into my arms afterward and comfort him. He had to continue to trust me to be his source of comfort and run to me instead of away from me.

The same is true with God and his children. Regardless of the age at which this happens to her, Jana may never understand why God allowed her father to suffer with cancer. From her vantage point, God stepping in and curing the cancer seems like the best and most godly solution. God won't explain himself to Jana, and adults shouldn't explain away his apparent inaction with platitudes like, "God's ways are not our ways." Instead, Jana and the adults in her life should focus on God's presence in the midst of everything Jana is going through. By focusing on experiencing God's presence with her, Jana can move to a position where God can be her source of comfort and strength. Jana needs to feel safe acknowledging her anger and confusion to God and be encouraged by adults to do this while she is positioned safely within his arms so he can comfort her and be in the midst of the awfulness with her.

God promises, "In this world you will have trouble" (John 16:33), but he also promises, "The LORD himself goes before you and will be with you; he will never leave you nor forsake you. Do not be afraid; do not be discouraged" (Deut. 31:8). When children experience the "trouble" God says will be present, they tend to ascribe responsibility to God and use it as evidence he has forsaken them and they're alone. As parents, we can be vessels of God's love who provide safe spaces for our child and encourage them to express their pain fully to God. As children mature, we can also invite them to grow in their understanding that this world is currently under the dictatorship of the enemy who seeks to "steal and kill and destroy," while Jesus came so they can "have life, and have it to the full" (John 10:10) even in the midst of troubles they experience. Parents need to help children understand *and* experience that, while God doesn't promise to remove their trouble, he does promise to be present with them and bring life in the midst of it. Jesus reminded his disciples, "Are not two sparrows sold for a penny? Yet not one of them will fall to the ground outside your Father's care. And even the very hairs of your head are all numbered" (Matt. 10:29–30). He doesn't promise the sparrow won't ever fall from the sky but rather it won't happen without the Father being present.

Increasing Awareness of God's Presence

Just like my son had to choose to reach out and allow me to scoop him up into my arms, children must practice being aware of God's presence with them and his provision for them. My son had to risk believing I would comfort him. When children choose to trust God is with them and will provide what they need, they risk as well. It is easy to focus on what isn't going the way children believe it should and more difficult to focus on God's presence in the midst of it.

The Hebrew view of time can be helpful in teaching children this practice. The Hebrew people viewed time as circular, just like they saw nature as circular—the moon follows the sun and day follows night, cyclically. Things that had happened could be counted on to happen again. Therefore, it was essential to understand what had happened in the past because it showed what could be counted on to happen in the future.[4] The Hebrew people retold the stories of God's faithfulness and, as a result, expected to encounter this same faithfulness in their current circumstances. Whenever they took their eyes off his past faithfulness, they quickly became overwhelmed by their circumstances and began to doubt his presence with them. When we help our child regularly rehearse ways God has been faithful to them, it reminds them of his presence with them amid their current circumstances—even when these circumstances are painful and difficult. This habit of rehearsing God's past faithfulness helps children to look for and expect the same faithfulness and provision they have experienced in the past in their current circumstances.

Children experience God faithfully providing what they need, but most children don't spend time rehearsing the stories of his provision. To build an enacted belief of God's faithfulness, they need to change this! Scripture gives us a framework in Paul's teaching:

> Let the peace of Christ rule in your hearts, since as members of one body you were called to peace. And be thankful. Let the message of Christ dwell among you richly as you teach and admonish one another with all wisdom through psalms, hymns, and songs

from the Spirit, singing to God with gratitude in your hearts. And whatever you do, whether in word or deed, do it all in the name of the Lord Jesus, giving thanks to God the Father through him. (Col. 3:15–17)

It is easy to read this and interpret it to mean "good" Christians are thankful for even the bad things in their lives. Unfortunately, many parents (including me, in the past) teach children it isn't okay to be upset with God when things don't go well. This is not what Paul intended. His words admonish us to spend time with our child every day looking for the ways God has been with them and is taking care of them. Some days this is easy to see, and other days it is more difficult to see God's faithful provision. However, even in the most awful situation, God is still with them and still taking care of them. Actively looking for and keeping a record of God's activity in our child's life helps them construct an enacted belief of God as trustworthy and willing to provide what they need amid whatever they are facing. Building and rehearsing an awareness of God's provision and presence is how children "put legs under" Paul's admonishment to be thankful in everything.

Scripture is replete with stories of God's presence and provision intermingled with the distressed cries of his people begging him to provide what they need. The key is helping children to

- Recount the evidence of his provision and faithfulness.
- Allow him to comfort them in their distress.

When children honestly and completely share their deepest pain with God *and* believe he will provide exactly what they need to get through today, they can confidently and competently live without being overwhelmed by fear and anxiety.

If you read the last sentence carefully, you will notice I didn't say they *won't* experience fear or anxiety but that fear and anxiety won't consume them. Moment by moment, God will get children through each day by being present with them and giving them the manna they need for the moment they are in—no matter how painful it might be.

Parenting to Increase Awareness of God's Presence

Children need experiences of God's presence. Below are several ideas to get you started.

Practice safe-place prayer. The safe-place prayer discussed in chapter 7 provides a way to help children move toward God when they are upset and afraid. This prayer doesn't require them to banish their negative emotions but invites them to experience the presence of God, share whatever is on their mind with him, and allow God to respond.

Listen for God's response with your child and gently intervene if your child's experience begins to run contrary to Scripture. For example, if your child tells God how mad they are about being bullied on the playground and believes God responds by telling them they deserved it because they are dumb, intervene. Depending on the age of your child, you might respond by saying, "I know you heard you got what you deserved because you are dumb, but I don't think that is God. It might sound like God, but remember how we talked about God never saying anything different from what the Bible says? Well, the Bible says to talk to others in ways that help and encourage them, not in ways that tear them down (Eph. 4:29). This means God would never say you deserved to be taunted or called names. I wonder if those words are the things you were worried God thinks about you. When I was listening for God's response as you were praying, I heard God saying, 'He heals the brokenhearted. He bandages their wounds' (Ps. 147:3 ICB). Could you ask God to show you how he wants to bandage your wounds and see what happens?" If your child is older, have them check Scripture to see if it lines up with what they were hearing as they prayed.

Having your child pour out their feelings to God and then listen for how he responds to them can provide profound healing to your child's heart and mind. As your child prays, intercede by asking for God's presence to be real to them and for the enemy's voice to be silenced so they can hear from their Father.

Tell the stories. Teach your child the stories of God's faithfulness. Spend time reading Bible stories of God's faithfulness to his people. Talk through how God took care of his people in the story and look for ways God has done the same thing for your child. For example, as you read about God parting the Red Sea so the Israelites could get away from the people who were picking on them and trying to hurt them, you can help your child identify times when God provided a way for them to get away from an annoying sibling or kids on the playground who were picking on them. Consider creating a journal to describe the ways God takes care of your child each day. Record what you see, in addition to the ways your child identifies God's care. Write in the journal every day and review what you have recorded once every week or two. As you read back through the journal, take time to pray with your child and thank God for the things the two of you have seen him do as well as the ways he provided protection that went unseen.

Create a symbolic reminder. When the Israelites crossed the Jordan River at last, God directed them to pick up stones from the middle of the river to build an altar reminding them what he had done. Throughout Scripture, God provided tangible reminders to help his people remember who they were and who he was—and is. Together with your child, consider picking something small your child can carry with them to remind them God is with them and taking care of them. Ideally this will be something they can carry in their pocket or place where they'll see it frequently. Each time your child sees or feels this object, have them take a moment to remind themselves, *God is with me right now. He is more real than this object. I can trust him to take care of me for the rest of today.*

≡ *Applying What You Learned*

Having a growth mindset and the ability to trust God are essential elements in taming worry and anxiety. Belief systems are extremely powerful, and changing them requires repeated experiences that are more powerful than the experiences that created the original beliefs.

1. Which aspects of changing your child's mindset or beliefs seem like they would be the most difficult for you to implement? What is something you can do to help with these areas?

2. Pick one aspect of parenting for a growth mindset you want to improve and develop a plan to monitor for this skill. One of my strategies for developing new parenting techniques was to hang an index card on the refrigerator and make a hash mark on it every time I engaged in the behavior I was attempting to develop. The goal is to build skills, and this means you will need a lot of practice. Plan to practice this skill for at least twenty-one consecutive days. Once you are able to consistently utilize this skill, go back to the list and pick another skill to work on.

3. This chapter listed several activities your child can engage in to build their awareness of God's presence and provision for them. Talk with your child about these activities and make a plan together for beginning the process of implementing one of them. You can't make your child do anything, so approach this as a team effort.

ELEVEN

Taming Anxious Thoughts

When children live out of healthy belief systems, they experience fewer anxious thoughts. However, anxiety isn't always unhealthy, so even the healthiest of belief systems won't eliminate all anxious thoughts. Children with anxiety disorders tend to operate out of unhealthy belief systems and also tend to have more anxious thoughts than other children their age. They need to be able to identify what they are thinking and stop the anxious thoughts from setting off the cascade of anxious feelings that in turn lead to anxious behaviors.

If thirteen-year-old Malek has a test at school, anxious thinking might create this cascade:

Anxious Thought	Anxious Feeling	Anxious Behavior
• This is awful. I'm going to fail this test.	• Scared • Anxious • Worried	• Obsessive studying instead of going to bed • Crying • Refusing to go to school

Compare Malek's experience to that of Melissa, who faces the same test with thoughts that are not as anxious:

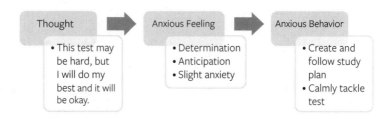

Thought		Anxious Feeling		Anxious Behavior
• This test may be hard, but I will do my best and it will be okay.		• Determination • Anticipation • Slight anxiety		• Create and follow study plan • Calmly tackle test

Notice Melissa still experiences some anxiety. The difference is her anxiety doesn't overwhelm her and lead to negative behaviors. For Melissa, knowing she has a test prompts mild anxiety, which motivates her to study and to apply herself when the test is handed to her.

The goal of this chapter is *not* to eliminate your child's anxious thoughts but to manage their intensity and use them to prompt helpful behaviors.

Identifying Thoughts

Children don't necessarily understand they have the ability to steward what they think. In fact, children are rarely aware of what they are thinking. The first step in helping children manage anxious thoughts is to help them identify their thoughts. When I explain this to children, I often start by explaining God created our brain to produce hundreds of thoughts in a minute. Our brain, like Aggie the lion, must be brought under our control, or trained, so it helps us. Training our thoughts is a job God gave us. Training thoughts—just like training a lion—is something we must learn how to do. Children aren't born knowing how to control their arms, their legs, or their brain—but they are born learners. I often spend time with children looking with them at all the things they have learned to control about their body so far in their life. It can be fun and affirming for children and adolescents to look at how much they have mastered by their current life stage. The younger the child, the more this list must be tangible. For example, I would have five-year-old Camilla sit with me and think about all the things babies can't do that she can do. Then we would look at all the things Camilla couldn't do before she went to kindergarten and has learned to do since she started school. By the end, we would have a paper filled with things Camilla has learned to do in her five years of life. Once we have celebrated how good she has been at learning new things over the last five years, it is then time to provide some basic information about thoughts.

I describe thoughts as the words we say silently to ourselves in our head. Thoughts *only* occur in our head, so others don't know what we are thinking and don't normally think exactly the same things we are thinking. Sometimes the thoughts in our head are helpful and based on things that are true. Other times the thoughts in our head are not helpful or are based on things that are false.

Because children learn best through experience, I then tell Camilla I am going to set something on the table in front of her, and she is going to listen for all the thoughts she has in her head when I do this while I do the same. I put a candy bar or a toy on the table and wait for about thirty seconds. We then make a list of all the thoughts Camilla had. Her list might include things like:

- I wonder what Jean is going to put on the table.
- I hope it is something fun.
- Oh, it's a candy bar.
- I love Twix.
- I wonder if she is going to let me have the candy bar.

I share my list of thoughts as well, and we talk about how two people can have different thoughts around the same thing. Then we go back and talk over how the thoughts on her list made her feel. Camilla might identify she felt a little scared when she thought

187

about what I might be going to put on the table and worried it might be something bad (another thought we add to her list). When she saw the Twix, she felt happy because she likes candy bars. The thought I might give her the candy bar created a feeling of excitement for her. A conversation like this gives us a wonderful way to talk about how thoughts create feelings.

Younger children have a diffi-cult time understanding the dif-ference between thoughts and feelings, so practice identifying thoughts and feelings. One way to do this is to look at pictures of people doing different things and make a list of all the different things they might be thinking.

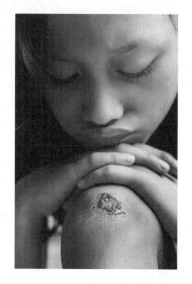

Six-year-old Stephen might look at the image to the right and identify, "She's sad," which is a feeling, not a thought. Practice helping your child generate different thoughts and distinguishing between thoughts and feelings until they can do this consistently. It can be helpful for younger children to think of thoughts as starting in their head and feelings as starting in their body—often their stomach.

For older children, have them take five or ten minutes each day to just write everything that comes into their head without filter-ing. Then, have them go back through their writing and cross out the feelings so they are left with the thoughts.

Identifying Feelings

Once your child is successfully able to identify thoughts, the next step is to begin identifying how different thoughts create different feelings. In the image above, Stephen might identify the child in the picture is thinking,

- I hope Mom isn't mad at me.
- I can't believe I fell down again.

The next step is to help Stephen generate feelings these thoughts might create. The list of feeling words in appendix C can be helpful as children begin identifying feelings. Narrow this list to words appropriate for the age of your child. Appendix D contains a chart of faces for different emotions, which may work better for younger children. Stephen might decide:

Practice identifying the difference between thoughts and feelings as well as the connection between them. Once they can do this proficiently, it is time for your child to begin practicing this skill with their own thoughts—particularly their anxious thoughts.

Identifying Anxious Thoughts: Wall of Worry

Anxious children tend to see the world as threatening or dangerous, so their thoughts focus on the things that might go wrong. The first step in taming these thoughts is identifying the anxious thoughts your child is having. Children who aren't normally talkative may simply feel anxious and not have any idea what thought creates this feeling. If you have a child who has this experience, don't press them or offer possibilities, as this can create anxious thoughts that weren't there previously. Instead, focus on the events that are anxiety-provoking to them.

One way to help children identify anxious thoughts and events is to construct a "Wall of Worry." It can be helpful to construct this on the inside of a closet door that can be closed or on a sheet of butcher paper that can be rolled up when not in use. You will eventually need four different colors of sticky notes, but for now, two will suffice. Using the first color, have your child list situations where they find themselves worrying or feeling anxious and write each one on a separate sticky note. Your child might list things like:

- Taking a test.
- Eating school lunch.
- Having parents not come home on time.
- Being called on in class.
- Driving a car.
- Going on a date.
- Doing things I have never done before.

Then, have your child arrange these events on the wall with the most anxiety-provoking at the top and the least anxiety-provoking at the bottom.

Next, move to thoughts that create anxiety. Using the second color of sticky note, have your child list worry thoughts they have. Some children will rattle off worry thoughts easily, while

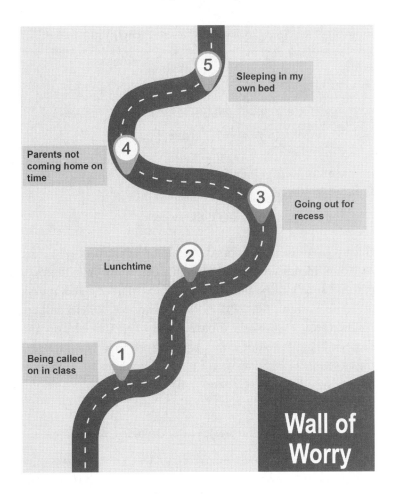

others will struggle. If your child finds it difficult to identify worry thoughts, validate this and plan to work together as detectives to see if you can uncover worry thoughts. Then watch for times when they appear worried and ask what they are thinking. Write down the thoughts they identify so they can be added to the wall later.

Have your child place their worry thoughts on the Wall of Worry next to the events where they have those thoughts. You may need to write the same thought on multiple sticky notes so they can place it next to several different events. Your child might have worry thoughts like:

- I'm going to fail the test.
- People are going to laugh at me if I make a mistake.
- I'm going to die if I keep feeling like this.
- I'm an idiot.
- This is never going to work out.
- What if Dad gets in an accident?
- I'm going to get sick and throw up.

When you have identified worry thoughts for each anxiety-producing situation, identify the worry thoughts that show up in multiple places. Circling those thoughts with a red marker makes it easy to see the pattern. This Wall of Worry becomes the place where children store their worry thoughts and where they identify the thoughts they are going to work on as they move forward. Closing the closet door or rolling up the paper helps them put the worry thoughts away and go on to their next activity.

Labeling Thoughts Accurately: Facts, Opinions, or Feelings

Thinking something doesn't make it true. One way to help younger children understand this is to place a small object in a box (without your child seeing what it is) and then wrapping the box. Put this "gift" on the table and have your child make a list of the things they think about the gift. Their list might look like this:

- That is pretty wrapping paper.
- I hope it's for me.
- I hope it isn't a dinosaur, because that would be a lame gift.
- It would be really cool if that box was full of candy and Mom gave it all to me!

Once they have generated their list, read through it together and ask them, "Can all of these thoughts be true?" Using the list above, you might ask, "Do you think it can be a dinosaur *and* candy? Is it possible none of these thoughts are true? Is it possible one of these thoughts is true?" Talk about how God created their brain to think thoughts all day, but not all of these thoughts are facts. Part of maturing is to test thoughts to determine which are facts, which are opinions, and which are feelings. Ask your child how they can determine which thoughts about the gift are facts. They will likely identify opening the gift as the only way to know. Have your child open it and, once they know its contents, go back through their thought list to identify the facts, opinions, and feelings. Using the list above, you might identify:

- "That is pretty wrapping paper" represents an opinion (not everyone would think the wrapping paper is pretty).
- "I hope it's for me" represents a feeling (hope is a feeling).
- "I hope it isn't a dinosaur, because that would be a lame gift" represents an opinion (not everyone would consider a dinosaur to be a lame gift).
- "It would be really cool if that box was full of candy and Mom gave it all to me" represents an opinion (not everyone would believe this was cool).

Opinions and feelings are not wrong but shouldn't be labeled as facts. Fear is a feeling. When we treat an opinion or a feeling as a fact, we give it more power than it should have. For example, if fifteen-year-old Jasmine sees two girls whispering in the hall, she might think, *They're talking about me and they hate me.* Jasmine has two thoughts:

- They are talking about me.
- They hate me.

Having those thoughts isn't wrong, but it doesn't make them facts. If Jasmine treats these thoughts as facts, she will go through her day believing these two girls have been talking about her and hate her. This will create worry about what they are saying about her, why they are talking about her, why they hate her, and how she is going to survive at school with people saying bad things about her. Treating these two thoughts as facts will create a lot of anxiety for Jasmine! However, if she is able to label her thoughts as fearful feelings, she can then work to check for the facts.

Checking for "Just the Facts"

Our brain generates fearful thoughts to keep us safe. Because our brain is attempting to make sure we don't get hurt, it tends to assume the worst and generates a lot of fearful thoughts. This is like Aggie roaring at anything that could potentially hurt him. He roars at little sounds he hears, anything that comes near his cage, and anyone or anything that enters his cage—even his trainer. Aggie's trainer has to help Aggie know which things will hurt him and which things won't. In the same way, our job is to identify which thoughts are fearful thoughts and then to look at the facts to determine how real the danger is. When Jasmine identifies her thoughts as fearful thoughts, she can begin to check out the facts. What she would find is:

- Two girls are looking in my direction.
- Two girls are whispering to one another.

Those are the facts. She doesn't have any evidence the girls' whispering or looking in her direction is about her, and she doesn't have any way of knowing what others feel about her unless they tell her.

I often describe checking for "just the facts" as being a good detective. Detectives look for the facts to solve mysteries. They don't get to decide who the burglar is without finding the evidence that proves it first. Dealing with fearful thoughts requires being good detectives who expertly determine what the facts are.

Practice this in multiple situations to help your child gain skill in identifying facts and separating facts from fearful thoughts. Play detective by identifying different thoughts you have, then ask your child to help you determine which ones are facts, which ones are opinions, and which ones are fearful thoughts. Read books with your child and identify the factual thoughts versus the opinions and fearful thoughts the characters have. Talk about things friends or teachers say to your child and identify the facts, opinions, and fearful thinking in these statements.

Once your child is proficient at identifying the difference between factual thoughts, opinions, and fearful thoughts, go back to the Wall of Worry. Start at the bottom and look at the thoughts associated with the lowest event on the wall. On each sticky note, identify whether the thought is a fact, opinion, or fear. This may be difficult for your child, as fearful thoughts often feel like facts! For example, if Zack identified "going out for recess" on his Wall of Worry, he might have thoughts like this:

These thoughts may feel like facts to Zack; however, these are things Zack fears. Once Zack identifies them as fears, it's time to check for "just the facts." He might identify the following as facts connected to going out for recess:

- Everyone goes outside for recess unless they have an excuse.
- Some children play alone at most recesses.
- Some children rarely play alone at recess.
- Not everyone gets made fun of at recess.
- I have asked my friend to play with me at recess, and they said yes.
- I have been asked to play by other people at recess sometimes.

None of these facts guarantee Zack won't be left out, have to play alone, or be made fun of at recess. However, identifying the facts helps alleviate some of the fear that occurs when fearful thoughts are treated as facts. Be careful not to invalidate your child's fear but rather help them identify the facts.

Using this pattern, work with your child to identify the facts around each of the situations on the bottom part of their Wall of Worry. Don't try to do all of the situations on their wall. It is better to stay low on the wall and allow your child to experience success at labeling fearful thinking and identifying facts. As your child goes through their week, look for places where the events at the bottom of their wall occur during their day. If they are able to identify facts or fearful thinking, talk about what they have learned. Using Zack's example of going out for recess, he might end up with a Wall of Worry that looks like this:

Types of Fearful Feeling Thoughts

Our brain attempts to keep us safe by generating fearful thoughts, just like Aggie attempts to keep himself safe by roaring. Aggie's roars can be categorized as loud roars, soft roars, or medium roars. Similarly, there are patterns to the fearful thoughts our brain produces. Let's look at four common types.

Forecasting

When you watch the weather on TV, the forecaster is taking pieces of data and using those pieces of data to predict tomorrow's

197

weather. Our brain sometimes functions like a weather forecaster. It takes pieces of data and puts them together to predict what will happen in the future. However, unlike a weather forecaster who is trying to accurately predict what will happen, our brain attempts to predict the worst thing that might happen to make sure we are prepared. When our brain is in forecaster mode, it looks at a situation, thinks about what might go wrong, and then predicts those things *will* go wrong. Not only does our brain predict those things *will* go wrong, but it also predicts we *won't* be able to cope when they happen. So, just like Aggie forecasts his trainer is going to hurt him when he enters the cage, Zack's brain forecasts he will be alone and be picked on at recess. If we investigated further, we might find Zack's brain also forecasts he won't be able to cope if this happens. Other examples of forecasting include:

- I'm going to mess this up—I know it!
- No one will help me.
- I'm going to be anxious if I do this.

All-or-Nothing Thinking

When our brain engages in all-or-nothing thinking, it looks at the extremes—something is either good or bad, perfect or a total failure. All-or-nothing thinking tends to include words like *always* or *never*. In reality, most things fall in the middle, not the extremes. The ability to see middle ground develops along with your child's prefrontal cortex, so younger children have limited ability to do this. Additionally, when the brain moves into fight-flight-freeze, the prefrontal cortex's functioning is impaired making us less able to see middle ground. When our brain engages in all-or-nothing thinking, we may see one mistake as failure rather than seeing it as only one out of ten wrong, so an A grade overall. Examples of all-or-nothing thinking include:

- I always make mistakes.
- Dad told me to do my homework before I watched TV, but I forgot, so Dad is going to hate me and I'm never going to get my homework done.
- I was anxious thinking about going to school, so I'm never going to be able to manage my feelings.

Mind Reading

Our brain wants to ensure we avoid situations where we might get hurt. One of the ways it does this is by assuming it knows what others think. Just like forecasting, when our brain engages in mind reading, it doesn't try to accurately predict thoughts or feelings but rather predicts the worst thing the individual might think or feel to prepare us. When Jasmine forecasts the two girls are talking about her, she then mind-reads and assumes they are talking about her because they feel hatred toward her. The problem with mind reading is that no one, except God, knows what others think or feel. Examples of mind reading include:

- He thinks I'm stupid.
- She doesn't like me.
- You hate me.

Overestimating the Odds

Younger children's brains have less capacity to accurately determine the likelihood of something happening. Additionally, when engaged in fearful thinking, our brain tends to overestimate or ignore the likelihood of something happening. This often happens for children around things like death and illness. When a child is overestimating the odds, they feel a gurgle in their stomach and are sure they are going to throw up. Other examples include:

- Mom is ten minutes late getting home, and I know she has been in an accident.
- I'm going to faint in front of the class.
- I'm going to get sick from eating this.

Categorizing Fearful Thoughts

Once your child has learned to label their fearful thoughts, it is helpful to categorize them. Children of all ages can learn to do this, but you will need different strategies depending on the age of your child.

Younger Children

Younger children can learn to categorize thoughts by playing a game based on the card game Go Fish. To do this, take the different fearful thoughts your child identified on their Wall of Worry, plus those you've identified when reading books, watching shows, or talking about thoughts, and put each on an index card. Make the cards in pairs based upon the types of fearful thinking listed above. Deal four or six of the cards to each player (depending on the age of the player and the number of cards you have). Players attempt to obtain pairs of cards with the same type of fearful thought and lay them down to empty their hand. So, if I have a card with the fearful thought "I'm going to die," I ask another player if they have an "overestimating the odds" card. If they have a card with that type of fearful thought, they must give it to me. If not, they tell me to "Go fish," I draw a card from the draw pile, and the next player's turn begins. When I get two "overestimating the odds" cards, I lay them down and announce the type of pair I am laying down, and the other players confirm I am correctly labeling the cards. The first person to lay down all their cards wins. Keep adding cards to the deck as new fearful thoughts are identified and play the game to refine your child's ability to identify fearful thinking. You can make the game more interesting by also adding pairs of factual thoughts like, "Two girls are talking in the hallway," or "My stomach made a gurgling sound."

Older Children/Adolescents

If your child is old enough to roll their eyes at the thought of a card game, they can still learn to categorize fearful thoughts. This is their process, so you can't dictate what they "have" to do. It helps older children know they aren't "freaks" or "childish" if you also work to identify your fearful thoughts while they work to identify theirs. I sometimes have tweens and teens create a checklist or spreadsheet to help them monitor their thoughts. They might end up with a sheet that looks like this:

Thought	They're talking about me. They hate me.
Is this thought a fact?	No
What is the evidence?	• Two girls whispering while looking down the hallway. • I'm standing in part of the hallway where they are looking. • Many other students are standing around me in the same part of the hall.
Is this thought an opinion?	No
Is this thought a fear?	Yes
Forecasting?	Yes—Took two pieces of data and made it about me.
All or Nothing?	No
Mind Reading?	Yes—I can't know for sure what they feel about me.
Overestimating the Odds?	Potentially—they might be looking at me but the odds of this are small.

Focus on Helpful Thoughts

Our brains attempt to protect us by generating thoughts about what might happen. This doesn't keep bad things from happening or equip us to effectively deal with them. I talk about this by putting a hammer, board, and nail on the table and telling the child I want to hammer the nail into the board. As I hold the nail with one hand and prepare to hit it with the hammer, I look at the child and say, "Wait! Is there a chance I might hit my finger with the hammer?" Most children will agree this is something that might happen. I then lay my hand on the table, raise the hammer, and prepare to hit my thumb. I ask, "If I hit my finger with the hammer now, will it prepare me to handle the pain if I hit my finger with the hammer later when I'm pounding in the nail?" Most children adamantly argue this won't help me and will just make my finger hurt ahead of time. Some children will tell me I should hit my finger to be prepared, and that answer creates an opportunity to talk about why they think this and to guide them to a place where they understand hitting my finger with the hammer would increase my current pain and not make me more equipped to deal with a future pain. Then we talk about what will help me if I do accidentally hit my finger. Most children will identify things I should do to help my finger feel better. This creates a conversation about the fact I have the skills to handle the situation if it were to happen, so I can wait to see if it happens and know I will be able to deal with it.

Walking through this example is extremely helpful and, while adolescents don't need props, the same example is useful in helping them identify that inflicting pain ahead of time "in case" is not effective. We then discuss how worrying about what might happen is the emotional equivalent of hitting your finger with the hammer ahead of time in case you slip and miss the nail later. Fearful thoughts don't equip us to make sure bad things don't happen or help us better handle them if they do happen.

Next, we look at what type of thoughts might actually be helpful. With younger children, I return to my hammer and nail and ask them what thoughts will help me carry out my task successfully. We look at thoughts like, "Make sure you keep your hand steady and don't get distracted" as helpful thoughts that will increase my chances of success. Identifying helpful thoughts and focusing on them helps us be successful and experience less anxiety. Once your child understands this, it is time to begin identifying helpful thoughts and looking at ways to focus on them. Go back to the Wall of Worry and the fearful thoughts your child identified connected to events at the bottom of the wall. Remember Zack's worry thoughts connected to recess? Zack might identify helpful thoughts like these:

These thoughts will help Zack cope with situations that don't go the way he wants *and* help him cope with anxiety he may experience related to what might go wrong.

As your child identifies helpful thoughts they can use to cope with anxiety or fearful thinking, write them on the third color sticky note and add them to the wall. Once Zack identifies helpful thoughts he can use, I would have him imagine he is getting ready to go out for recess and describe what he sees. As he describes this, I would ask him how he feels. He may describe anxious feelings, or he may not. If he doesn't identify feeling anxious, I would say, "What would happen if you begin to think some of your fearful thoughts about going out to recess?" He would likely identify these thoughts as creating anxiety, and we would then discuss how he can "talk back" to his anxious thoughts using helpful thoughts. He might say, "These are anxious thoughts. They aren't facts. They are trying to keep me safe, but they don't really protect me. If I go out for recess and no one plays with me, I can play by myself. I can't make someone ask me to play, but I can ask Josh to play ball with me and see what he says." Zack would rehearse this scene in his head until he can consistently talk back to the thoughts. We may even create an index card or a picture to help him remember how he will talk back to these fearful thoughts when he hears them.

Zack is now ready to try this skill out in real life. I would remind him his mind is really good at thinking fearful thoughts, so he will need to repeatedly practice shifting his mind from fearful thoughts to helpful thoughts so his mind becomes good at this new process. We would talk about the importance of strengthening his mind's "helpful thoughts" muscle. Every morning, Zack should rehearse using his helpful thoughts successfully as he gets ready to go out for recess. He will then practice them at school and talk about how it went when he gets home that night.

I would reinforce progress toward consistently utilizing helpful thoughts and remind Zack the goal isn't getting rid of all anxiety but taming his thoughts so he can direct them. We might watch videos of lion trainers teaching lions to normalize this as a process that takes time. It is important for children to understand that the goal is having the ability to direct thoughts, not eliminate all anxiety, and this will take practice. Reinforcing effort rather than perfection is crucial.

☰ *Applying What You Learned*

Helping children learn to tame their thoughts is an important part of managing worry and anxiety and requires repeated experiences that are more powerful than the experiences that created the original thought patterns.

1. As you read the chapter, which parts of learning to tame fearful thoughts seemed most applicable to where your child is right now? Talk with your child about working on this area. Your child's choice matters, so check with them to see what they are willing to try.

2. This chapter listed several activities your child can engage in to build their awareness of thoughts, their fearful thoughts, and how they can use helpful thoughts to challenge fearful thoughts. Talk with your child about these activities and make a plan together to begin implementing one of these activities. Approach this as a team effort!

TWELVE

Taming Anxious Feelings

My children experienced the loss of their father when they were young. This created emotional pain for them and for me. I desperately wanted my children to become healthy adults who loved God, operated from the knowledge they were deeply loved, and leveraged their gifts and talents to positively influence the world around them. I attempted to parent in ways that facilitated this outcome. One series of parenting memories etched in my memory emanates from hearing my children share their intense, pervasive longing to have a father like their friends. They would tearfully talk about the pain of having lives different from other children. I would listen and feel their pain colliding with my own, resulting in an overwhelming emotional intensity that rolled over me. After listening, I consistently replied, "God always gives us what we need but he doesn't promise to give us what we want."

At the time, my response felt like good parenting. I was teaching my children truths about God and how he functioned with his children. However, looking back, I deeply regret those parenting moments! My fear that my children's loss would inhibit their development, combined with my own grief and loss, created the ideal breeding ground for invalidating my children's emotional experiences. I responded with a truth about God while also, unfortunately, telling them to *stop feeling* because they had what they needed. My behavior invalidated their emotions and was harmful to them. As I grew to understand this, I needed to seek God's forgiveness, acknowledge my hurtful behavior to my children, and ask their forgiveness.

I share this example from my life for two reasons:

1. To help parents identify ways they may inadvertently invalidate their child's feelings out of their own discomfort or desire to ensure their child's healthy development.
2. So parents know that, even when they are doing the best they know to do, they can hurt their child. The key is to own mistakes and seek the forgiveness of God and our child when this happens.

Adults in a child's world tend to invalidate the child's feeling if the feeling seems larger than the situation warrants or if the child is not managing the feeling in ways the adult believes they should. Statements like "It isn't that big of a deal" tell a child their feelings aren't appropriate or understood and leave the child feeling alone, ashamed, and unseen. When a child's emotions are invalidated, the child is left with two options: pushing the emotions down to make them go away or sitting in their emotions feeling ashamed for having them and ill-equipped to manage them.

Pushing emotions down is like pushing a beach ball underwater. It takes a ton of energy to hold a beach ball underwater. You inevitably run out of the strength and will to keep pushing it down. When the ball is released, it capitalizes on the energy you gave it by pushing it down and pops up with more force than it had when you pushed down. Emotions don't go away when they're pushed down. Instead, they show up somewhere else with more intensity than before.

When my daughter pushed down her sadness about not having a father in her life, it took energy to hold those sad feelings down. She would successfully hold the feelings at bay until something stressed the system—like getting excluded at recess. All of a sudden, she no longer had the energy to hold her original emotion down *and* deal with her current situation. Her original emotion popped back to the surface, attached itself to the pain of not being picked by her friends, and resulted in her crying inconsolably for hours. The cycle only intensified when I, not understanding what was happening, saw her reaction as being larger than life and told her she was overreacting. Once again, her emotions were invalidated, leaving her to either push them back down or sit in them alone, feeling ashamed. A cycle of invalidation like this creates an environment where children are unable to own, process, and develop skills for effectively managing emotions.

In this chapter, we will look at the function of feelings and skills children can use in response to their feelings.

Validating Emotions

Feelings are neither right nor wrong—feelings simply are. This may be difficult to comprehend, but it's true. Children feel, and their feelings aren't good or bad, right or wrong—they *are*. Accepting and understanding this is the first step to validating your child's emotional experience. While emotions are not right or wrong, what is done with them can be helpful or unhelpful. Our job, as parents, is to teach our child how to respond to their emotions in helpful ways. To do this, we must acknowledge what they're feeling and help them do the same.

Acknowledging feelings doesn't mean agreeing with what our child is feeling. Acknowledging simply means working to understand what they're feeling. This can be difficult when we don't like what they're feeling or when their feelings resonate with or intensify something we're feeling. My children had intense feelings of sadness, longing, loss, and isolation connected to the loss of their father. They, like all people, needed an empathic witness—someone who would hear their emotions, validate their experience, and let them know they were not alone in the experience. They shared their experience with me hoping I would meet them in their pain, acknowledge that their feelings made sense given their experiences, and reassure them I would journey with them to figure out how to deal with these feelings.

Every human being needs empathic witnesses, including Jesus. When Jesus went into the garden of Gethsemane, he took three disciples with him. He asked them to be present and shared his emotions with them: "My soul is very sad and deeply grieved, so that I am almost dying of sorrow" (Matt. 26:38 AMPC). Then he invited them to be present as he processed his emotions by saying, "'Stay here and keep watch with me.' Going a little farther, he fell with his face to the ground and prayed" (vv. 38–39). He invited them to hear his pain and his conversation with God. He welcomed their presence and wanted them to understand what he was feeling. The disciples, like many of us, didn't get it and were so consumed by what was happening for them that they were unable to be present for Jesus.

Thankfully, we have a God who is the perfect empathic witness and models for us how to do this with our child. God hears our pain and meets us where we are. He invites us to pour out our heart to him and promises he will be our refuge (Ps. 62:8). When he passed in front of Moses, he described himself as, "The LORD, the LORD, the compassionate and gracious God" (Exod. 34:6). David described God as someone who "is close to the brokenhearted and saves those who are crushed in spirit" (Ps. 34:18).

God invites us to receive comfort from him and then, from that experience, give the same sort of comfort to others. Jesus is described in 2 Corinthians 1:4 as the one "who comforts us in all our troubles, so that we can comfort those in any trouble with the comfort we ourselves receive from God." We are invited to be Jesus's hands and feet to our child by creating spaces where they experience what we have experienced with God. However, we can't do this if we haven't experienced him comforting us. Unprocessed pain in our own lives makes it difficult, if not impossible, to be empathically present with others in their pain. However, in places where we are attuned to God and our child, we can be vessels of God's love and compassion.

During their elementary school years, my children had summer babysitters while I was at work. My son loves adventure, so one summer he creatively decided to hide from the babysitter—routinely. This was entertaining for him but resulted in calls from a panicked babysitter that required me to leave work, drive home, and help uncover my son's latest hiding place. Finally, I laid down the ultimatum that if he hid from the babysitter one more time, he would have to sit in my office instead of going to the water park with his sister and the babysitter. My son vowed he wouldn't do it again and kept his promise . . . for a few days. Then I got another call saying he had gone missing. I made the trek home and, after searching for what felt like an eternity, he was discovered inside the washing machine (one of the old ones, with an agitator). After several frantic attempts to extract him without calling the fire department, we eventually extricated him (vegetable oil is a good thing!). I breathed a sigh of relief—and then sat down and calmly informed him he wouldn't be going to the water park. He sobbed and sobbed and promised to never hide again if he could just go. In that moment, I was able to sit with him, hold him, and say, "This stinks. I know how much you wanted to go and how sad it is you can't go." I just sat with him and let him be sad. No lectures. No reminders he created this mess. I was just present as he felt his feelings. Eventually, his tears stopped, and he relaxed into my arms and was still. He knew I got it. This didn't change the fact he spent the day with me at the office while his sister went to the water park, but it changed his emotional experience. He experienced someone understanding what he felt, being present with him, and comforting him in his sadness. That is what it means to be an empathic witness.

As parents, we need to be empathic witnesses for our child. To do this, we must hear their emotions, help them give language to their emotions, and be present with them as they express their emotions. We also have the opportunity to help our child *experience* God's presence in their emotions. One way to do this is to build onto the safe-place prayer we talked about in chapter 7. To do this, start by *being* the hands and feet of Jesus and just being present with your child until their emotions subside so they can engage. Then *ask* if they would like to pray.

If they are willing, the prayer process might look something like this: as the parent, you begin the prayer, saying, "Father, Son, and Holy Spirit, we know you are here. We ask that you flood this room with your presence and create a safe space where Kris can be with you. We ask that you cleanse Kris's imagination and use Kris's imagination to create a picture of safety."

After opening in prayer, allow time for God to create a picture and experience of safety for your child. Especially with younger children, have them describe their picture out loud. Once they have a picture where they feel safe, let them know they can invite Jesus to come and be present with them in their safe place whenever they are ready. When they are feeling safe in the presence of Jesus, invite them to share with him what they have been feeling. The goal would be for them to describe their emotions as vividly as they can to Jesus and then to watch and listen for how he responds to them.

Your role is to intercede over the space and to listen to what your child is experiencing. If it doesn't line up with the character of God or Scripture in some way, gently redirect your child. For example, if your eight-year-old child tells you Jesus told them their emotions were stupid, you might say, "I think that is something we might say to ourselves, but Jesus doesn't ever say bad things to people about what they are feeling. Jesus wept when his friend Lazarus died, and he wept when others were sad about his friend dying too. Jesus cares about what you are feeling, and he wouldn't tell you it was wrong to feel things. Let's ask him again what he thinks and feels about what you've told him." If your child is older, you might inquire about whether they believe what they just heard lines up with what Scripture says is true of Jesus and how he interacts with people. The goal is to gently redirect them back to Jesus and allow him to validate and comfort them in their experience.

Jesus wants to meet your child in their distress and be present with and comforting to them. When your child has experienced this, pray God would bless your child and continue to be their comfort, and allow your child to close the prayer when they are ready to be done.

The final step is to help your child validate their own emotions. Owning and validating their own emotions increases their ability to receive the comfort and care of others. Children (and adults!) often spend lots of time telling themselves they "shouldn't" be feeling what they feel. While this is done in an attempt to stop emotions that feel hurtful or overwhelming, it is ineffective and intensifies what they are feeling. When I talk with children about this, I use the illustration of pushing a beach ball underwater. For younger children, I will have them hold an actual beach ball underwater so they can see what happens. Then, we look at how telling ourselves we shouldn't feel doesn't make the feeling go away and often creates other negative emotions in addition to what we originally felt. We then practice labeling their feelings. Being able to label a feeling without acting on it or telling themselves it is wrong is the first step in managing the feeling. (Remember, appendix C contains a list of feeling words, and appendix D has faces depicting various feelings. These tools may be helpful as your child learns to label feelings.) Once your child understands the process, have them practice in non-anxiety-producing situations throughout their day.

As your child gains proficincy in labeling their emotions without judging them, go back to the bottom of their Wall of Worry and have them identify a situation they want to work on. Zack could use the diagram he has developed so far (like the one below) and begin to add in feelings.

Using a new color of sticky note, Zack would describe the feel-ings he experiences connected to the different thoughts he has. He might identify feelings like:

- I'm *scared* I will be all alone.
- I'm *optimistic* someone will ask me to play.
- I'm *sad* no one asked me to play last recess.
- I'm *excited* Josh asked me to play last week at recess.

There are no wrong feelings. Your job is to help your child give language to their feelings, not to tell them what they should or shouldn't feel. Talk about how normal it is for each thought to

create a feeling, and validate their feelings. Then invite them to label those same feelings as they encounter this situation in their daily life. Check in on how they do with this and encourage them to keep trying when they struggle.

Functions of Emotions

Feelings occur for a reason. Emotions are a nonverbal way our body and brain communicate information to us and to others. When Aggie roars, his roar communicates to others they need to back away. His roar is also his body's attempt to communicate something to him. Every emotion attempts to tell us something.

Emotions Communicate to Others

Emotions are a nonverbal way of communicating. When we are excited about the possibility of building a snowman, for example, others see our excitement and can "catch" it. Our emotions create emotions within others. The more intense our emotion, the more likely it is to impact others. Most children can identify a day when they woke up grumpy but, when they got to school and their friends were excited to see them, the grumpiness faded.

Emotions Communicate to Us

Just like emotions communicate to others, they also communicate to us. Some emotions are more pleasant than others, but each has a message. When Aggie roars, his body is attempting to tell him there might be danger nearby. The chart on the next page shows some common emotions and the messages these emotions are often attempting to communicate.

Identifying the Function of Emotions

Once your child can own and accurately label their emotions, it's time to identify the function of their emotions. Aggie's roar is his body's attempt to tell him (and everyone around him) something.

214

Love
- Tells us we care about someone or something
- Motivates investing time and care into relationship

Guilt
- Tells us we have done something inappropriate
- Motivates us to correct or fix what we have done

Anger
- Tells us we have been wronged or hurt
- Motivates us to change the situation

Sadness
- Tells us we have experienced a loss
- Motivates us to be with people who can comfort us

Fear
- Tells us there is potential danger
- Motivates us to protect ourselves from danger

Happiness
- Tells us something has gone well or was pleasant
- Motivates us to seek more of this sort of activity

The question is, What? Aggie might be roaring because his stomach growled, and he wants his trainer to know he is hungry. He might be roaring because his trainer just carried something new into his cage, and he is scared it might hurt him. For the trainer to help Aggie, the trainer needs to accept Aggie has roared without being upset or telling Aggie he shouldn't be roaring. Then Aggie's trainer will need to investigate to determine what made Aggie roar so he can decide what to do about it.

The same thing is true when our emotions "roar" at us. We need to determine what created the emotion by identifying the event that triggered it and our thoughts connected to that event. Then we investigate, like a detective, to see what the emotion is trying to communicate to us and to those around us. Once your child understands this concept, practice it with situations from books or shows your child watches. Have them identify an emotion a character is experiencing and explore what the emotion is attempting to communicate. You can also practice by telling your child about situations and emotions you experience and play detective together to identify what the emotions are attempting to tell you.

As they gain proficiency in identifying the function of emotions, begin having them identify the function of their own emotions. Start with pleasant emotions, as these have less emotional charge and your child will be less invested in avoiding the feeling. Finally, go back to their Wall of Worry and work to identify the function of the emotions they identified on the bottom of their wall. Zack might identify the following:

As your child identifies the potential function of each feeling, write those on the sticky note with the feeling.

Taming Feelings

Identifying the function of an emotion is the first step in successfully taming feelings. Just like lion trainers want lions to follow their commands rather than menacingly roaring, children can learn to manage emotions rather than being immobilized by the "roaring" of their emotions.

Emotions Are Time-Limited

Taming emotions requires children to understand emotions are attempting to tell them something *and* emotions are time-limited. In fact, just like Aggie's roar lasts for only a short period, most emotions only last for between thirty and ninety seconds.[1] This is a surprising fact for most children (and many adults). Younger children have little concept of time, so it can be helpful to equate the length of an emotion to a song. "Twinkle, Twinkle Little Star" sung start to finish at an average speed lasts around thirty seconds. Older children can benefit from finding songs that last either thirty, sixty, or ninety seconds. For example, the chorus of "Let It Go" from the movie *Frozen* is about thirty seconds. Remembering emotions are time-limited and singing their chosen song to themselves three or four times can help your child "ride the wave" of an emotion until it subsides.

Emotions have a short life—unless something happens to reignite or intensify them. To help your child understand this, strike a wooden match, lay it on a glass dish, and time how long it takes for the match to burn out completely. Write down the time. Then light a second match and lay it down in the same way. This time, feed little pieces of paper to the match to show how you can keep the fire burning with the same intensity for as long as you continue to feed it paper. Talk about what we might feed to our emotions to keep them burning. The goal is to help your child identify that thoughts and behaviors can feed emotions and keep them from "burning out."

After they identify this, light a third match, lay it on the glass dish, and this time crumple up some paper and lay it on top of the burning match to create a larger blaze. Talk about things we do that intensify emotions. Your child might identify the initial small fear of being called on in class and not knowing the answer as being intensified if they begin to rehearse all of the things their classmates might think about them if this happened.

Is the Message Accurate?

All emotions are attempting to tell us something, but their message is not always accurate or probable. We should listen to our emotions, acknowledge what they are attempting to tell us, and then evaluate the accuracy and probability of their message.

Suppose Timothy tells his friend he doesn't want to play with him at recess because he wants to play soccer and his friend is going to play basketball. His friend looks sad as he walks away, and Timothy feels guilty. Timothy identifies that his guilty emotion is telling him he may have done something wrong—maybe it was wrong to tell his friend no. Notice I said "may" have done something wrong. Emotions give us information we need to investigate to determine if it is a fact.

If Timothy acts upon his emotion without investigating to determine its truth, he treats the emotion as a fact, and this can cause problems. In this case, treating the guilt as evidence he shouldn't tell people no could cause Timothy to feel plagued by guilt whenever he considers saying no to someone. Left unchecked, he may become someone who capitulates to whatever the people around him want, regardless of whether it is healthy or something he really wants to do.

Timothy could also identify and name what he is feeling, look for the function of the feeling, and then check out the facts to see if this feeling is telling him something accurate or inaccurate. His internal dialogue might sound like this: *I just told Samuel I didn't want to play with him and now I have a pit in my stomach, and I feel guilty. Guilt, what are you trying to tell me? I think guilt is trying to tell me I shouldn't have told him no because I made him feel bad. Thank you, guilt, for alerting me to a potential mistake I need to check out.*

Once Timothy has identified the function of the guilt and validated the emotion, he is ready to check out the facts. The first thing Timothy must determine is what he controls and what belongs to others. Many intense and difficult to manage emotions are connected to attempting to control things that are not within our power. We can only manage our thoughts, our feelings, and our behavior. We don't have the ability or responsibility to control someone else's thoughts, feelings, or behavior. We also can't control the future or the past. Only God knows the future, and he doesn't give us what we need for the future until we get there. We can ask forgiveness for things we have done in the past, but we can't change the past. Ruminating about it drags the past into the present and overwhelms us.

One way of helping our child with this concept is by talking about managing their backyard. Children normally understand the concept of where their yard ends and the neighbor's yard begins. This makes it easy to talk about whether they can make their neighbor change what is in their backyard. Children may initially say they can make their neighbor comply. However, you can easily play this out with them until they conclude they can ask the neighbor to change their backyard but can't make them act upon the request. Children also understand they shouldn't go into their neighbor's backyard and take things without asking, because the things in their neighbor's backyard don't belong to them. They are in charge of the things in their backyard and need to take care of them but can't control what the neighbor does or what the neighbor has. Using this framework, you can help children identify what is theirs to control in a variety of situations.

Timothy might identify the following as he considers who has control of the different aspects of the situation:

Timothy	Stephen	God
• How I talked to Stephen • What I want to play at recess • What I feel • My choice to say yes or no	• His feelings • What he chooses to play at recess • If he plays with me next time	• What happens in the future between Stephen and me

This information will assist Timothy as he determines what the facts are surrounding the situation. He might identify this information:

- I answered Samuel's question honestly.
- I let Samuel know I like playing with him but want to play soccer instead of basketball this time.
- Samuel looked sad when I said no, and I feel bad about that, but it isn't my job to control what Samuel feels.
- It is okay to set limits and to say no to things, but that is hard for me to do and I don't like it.
- I'm worried that when I tell people no, they might not like me or want to play with me.

From this information, Timothy can identify he didn't do anything wrong, which should cause the guilt to dissipate. His guilt is related to Samuel's feelings combined with his fear about what Samuel might do in the future. Timothy's emotion alerted him to a potential problem. He looked at what it was trying to tell him and then used his "just the facts" skill to determine whether it was telling him something accurate or inaccurate. He concluded the emotion didn't fit the facts of the situation.

Often, the function of fear and anxiety is to alert us to potential danger. Children need to acknowledge this emotion and even thank their body for alerting them. Thanking their body validates that the emotion exists for a reason. It also allows them to begin stepping back from the emotion so they can engage the thinking part of their brain to assess the situation. It is like Aggie's lion trainer talking calmly to Aggie when he enters the cage. The lion trainer might quietly reassure Aggie, "I know you are scared because you don't know what is going to happen. It's okay." Calmly acknowledging the feeling helps avoid either fueling the emotion or attempting to push it away and get rid of it. Once the feeling has been acknowledged, your child can then begin looking for what the potential danger is.

Thirteen-year-old Whitney finds herself terrified every time she leaves for school. She worries something is going to happen to her mom while she is gone. She struggles to leave each day and insists upon texting her mom multiple times during the day. If her mom doesn't answer immediately, she panics and resorts to calling repeatedly until she is able to hear her voice and be reassured her mom is okay. With some coaching, Whitney begins to look for the function of her emotions. Eventually, she encounters her terror and responds by thanking her body for identifying something could potentially happen to her mother while she is at school. She is then ready to begin looking at what belongs in her backyard (is hers to control) and what is in other people's backyards. She might identify:

Whitney	Others	God
• My thoughts and feelings • Going to school and doing normal 13-year-old things there	• It is Mom's job to be sure she is making good choices that keep her safe	• Taking care of me if something happens to Mom • Taking care of Mom • What happens in the future

From here, Whitney is ready to begin looking for the facts surrounding this fear. The list she generates looks like this:

- In the thirteen years I have been alive, Mom has never been seriously harmed while I was at school.
- Worrying about Mom doesn't stop bad things from happening.
- Being with Mom won't necessarily stop bad things from happening.
- It is my job to trust God's plan for the future, not to try to control God's plan for the future.

As Whitney looks at her list, she can see two things:

- The thing she's worried about isn't something she has any control over.
- The thing she's worried about is unlikely although not impossible.

It's impossible to prove with 100 percent certainty that feared events won't happen. However, it is possible to see if fear is forecasting the worst possible outcome without looking at whether this is a *likely* outcome. In Whitney's case, nothing has happened to her mom in thirteen years, and her mom works to make healthy choices, so it's unlikely something awful will happen to her while Whitney is at school. The things Whitney is worried about aren't in her backyard, and worrying about them makes it difficult for her to control the things that *are* in her backyard.

Take examples from books, movies, or your life and work to identify with your child what's in the individual's backyard, others' backyards, and God's backyard. Then, have them identify whether the message the individual's emotion is attempting to communicate is accurate or not. When your child can proficiently do this, begin practicing with positive emotions in their life. As their skill level grows, it is time to go back to the Wall of Worry and practice this with the emotions they have identified on their wall. This is *very* difficult, so you will need to remain patient and affirming as they work on identifying what they have the power to control and how likely things are to happen.

Finding the Present Moment

God created human beings with five senses, and these senses only give data about what is going on in the current moment. The things we can see, hear, smell, touch, and taste are present things. Children can calm their emotions when they focus on what they can see, hear, feel, touch, and taste. Take a minute and try it with your child. Find a place for each of you to sit comfortably, and comfortably fix your gaze. Without moving anything (including your eyes), have each of you name five things you can see, five things you can hear, and five things you can physically feel (like your feet on the ground). Check with your child to see if this made them more aware of what was happening in the present moment and less aware of anxious or fearful thoughts and feelings.

Children's senses bring them into the current moment and make them aware of what is in that moment. The information children take in using their senses enters their brain through the limbic system. The limbic system (see diagram in chapter 1, on page 23) takes in the data and creates an emotional, instinctual response to this data. When children begin to describe what they observe, they begin to activate other areas of the brain that help balance the instinctual responses of the limbic system. Research shows attaching words to sensory experiences decreases the response of the amygdala (responsible for fight-flight-freeze) and increases activity in the ventrolateral prefrontal cortex (see diagram in chapter 2, on page 35).[2] This part of the brain suppresses instinctual responses and aids in making choices that help people accomplish their goals.[3] However, this process requires having words that accurately describe what is being observed.

As someone who talks with people all day and enjoys writing, I do not find it particularly difficult to find words to describe the desk I am sitting at: it is a light maple color with a simulated wood pattern, about sixty inches long, and is located facing a window that looks out onto a frozen drainage pond. The process of writing this last sentence caused me to focus my attention and think of words that fit my experience. It made me more aware of my desk and the view out my window, which increased my appreciation of both. However, this is not the case for many people—especially children. Children don't have mature language skills and may find it difficult to utilize descriptive language. Help your child find language to describe what they observe in the present moment as accurately as possible. The act of working to describe things slows their amygdala down, which makes emotions easier to manage.

Self-Soothing

As children become more aware of the present moment, they can also begin intensifying positive experiences in the present moment that are calming. This skill, called *self-soothing*, is something parents instinctually do for infants. Parents respond to a crying infant by rocking them, giving them a pacifier, singing to them, and/or swaddling them. Each of these activities intensifies the pleasure the infant can experience through one of their senses. Eventually many children learn to self-soothe on their own by sucking their thumb, holding a favorite blankie, or listening to a specific song when they're upset. Unfortunately, some children don't seem to naturally learn this. Other times, parents discourage these behaviors by labeling them as childish or unnecessary. While children need to modify these behaviors as they grow (it is probably not wise for a third grader to suck their thumb in class), everyone needs to learn age-appropriate, healthy ways to soothe themselves. Below are some ways to use each of the senses to calm anxiety or other painful emotions by intensifying positive emotions in the present moment.

See

- Go for a walk and describe as many things out loud as you can.
- Take a virtual museum tour and describe the parts of each exhibit you like the most.
- Find five different leaves you like and describe the differences between them.
- Light a candle and watch the flame.
- Look at pictures in a book you like.
- Watch a calming TV show.

Hear

- Listen to beautiful, soothing music.
- Listen to ocean sounds or sounds of nature.
- Listen to a parent read a story.

Smell

- See how many different smells you can find and name out loud.
- Light a scented candle and describe its smell.
- Put on scented lotion.
- Microwave popcorn or bake cookies and describe all of the smells involved.

Taste

- Take a favorite snack and divide it into small parts. See how long you can take to eat each part. Describe how it tastes and how it feels in your mouth as you eat each part.
- Have a tasting test. Taste different things and describe each in as much detail as you can. When you have tasted everything, pick your favorite and tell why you liked it.
- Have a cup of milk, juice, or hot chocolate. Hold each sip in your mouth and swish it around gently, then

swallow. When you have finished your drink, describe what you liked about it.

Touch

- Take a bubble bath.
- Take a cold shower.
- Put on a soft, fuzzy shirt or sweater and feel its softness.
- Cuddle up in a blanket (weighted blankets can be helpful for this).
- Rub lotion on your body slowly.
- Float in the tub or pool and feel the water around you.
- Pet the dog or cat and describe the feel of its fur.

Self-soothing is a set of skills that must be practiced regularly. Don't wait until your child is flooded with negative emotion and then have them try to self-soothe. Make self-soothing a regular part of every day and help your child identify a list of calming things. Use this list when emotions become intense.

≡ Applying What You Learned

Feelings are complex and extremely powerful. Changing them requires validating the feeling while also stepping back to evaluate what the feeling is attempting to communicate and whether this message is based upon facts.

1. As you read the chapter, which parts of learning to tame fearful emotions seemed most applicable to where your child is right now? Talk with your child about working on this area. It is important they *choose* to work on this, so don't tell them what they are going to do but talk to them about trying this out to see if it might be helpful.

2. Have your child pick an emotion they are experiencing (angry, anxious, happy, sad) and work to be only aware of everything associated with experiencing this emotion. Have them describe all the physical feelings they have in their stomach, shoulders, fingers, back, and other parts of their body as they feel this emotion. What are the thoughts associated with this emotion that they hear in their head? The goal is to observe every aspect of the emotion, not judge it.

3. This chapter lists several activities your child can engage in to build their awareness of what they feel and what the feeling is attempting to communicate to them and to evaluate these messages from their feelings. Talk with your child about these activities and make a plan together for beginning the process of implementing one of these activities. Approach this as a team effort!

4. Pick an activity you and your child do daily (making lunch, going for a walk, petting the dog, brushing your teeth), and work to be aware of everything that happens during the activity. As you do the activity or after you complete it, collaborate with your child to describe what you saw, heard, smelled, touched, or tasted.

5. While your child is eating something they enjoy, have them describe the experience of eating. What do they see connected to eating? What do they hear externally and internally as they eat? What does the substance feel like in their mouth? What does the utensil feel like in their hand? What do they smell? What are the tastes? Work to give language to each and every aspect of eating.

THIRTEEN

Taming Anxious Behavior

When a child is anxious, they become highly invested in avoiding whatever is creating anxiety—no matter the cost. Parents often become unwitting accomplices in an attempt to protect their child from intense negative emotion and to maintain some sense of normalcy within the home.

Children's Avoidant Behavior Patterns

Children have two basic patterns they utilize to avoid negative emotions. Some children *externally* do whatever it takes to avoid the situation. Others *internally* attempt to distract or dissociate from their emotions while going through the anxiety-producing event.

External Avoidance

If five-year-old Morgan is fearful she will eat something that will make her sick, she may restrict what she will eat down to peanut butter sandwiches made in front of her so she can be sure the knife and plate were clean. These parameters make family meals a nightmare, make it impossible to eat out, and create long-term health risks for Morgan. No amount of parental bribing, lecturing, punishing, or pleading will change Morgan's behavior. After exhausting all these options, her parents capitulate (as many do). Everyone in the family adapts their behavior to keep Morgan's anxiety at bay. While this makes life more manageable, it doesn't teach Morgan the skills necessary to manage her anxiety.

Internal Distraction

Sixteen-year-old Talal fears doing something wrong that will draw attention to him and instigate his peers' ridicule. He sits with a group of his friends at lunch and, while they chatter, mindlessly chews his sandwich while internally reliving the video game he played last evening. While his friends talk about what they will do after school, his mind is occupied with the video game battles he fought last night. He is at the lunch table but avoiding his anxiety by internally distancing himself from the anxiety-producing situation. Talal, like Morgan, has found a way to avoid the anxious feeling rather than learning skills to manage it.

Parents' Reinforcement Patterns

Avoidant behaviors (whether internal or external) only strengthen the thoughts and feelings that feed anxiety. Unfortunately, many parents reinforce avoidant behaviors by focusing their time and attention on the behavior. When a behavior receives attention, it is reinforced, and reinforcement increases the likelihood the behavior will reoccur. Behaviors can be positively or negatively reinforced, and parents often vacillate between the two.

Positive Reinforcement

Eight-year-old Paul demands that his father stay with him at his friend's sleepover for at least the first hour and be on call to come get him if he becomes scared and wants to leave. Paul's father wants his son to socialize so he agrees to these demands, hoping they will enable his son to feel comfortable. After sitting awkwardly with a group of eight-year-olds for an hour, he exits without being seen lest his son's anxiety be spiked by his leaving. All is well until 10:00 p.m., when he receives a panicked phone call from Paul demanding to be picked up because it is too scary to sleep at his friend's house. Knowing how frightened Paul is, his father promptly picks him up, comforts him, and settles him into his own bed for the night.

The attention Paul's father gives to Paul's anxiety reinforces that the anxiety is valid and should be attended to in ways that will make it hard for Paul not to demand the same response the next time he is away from home. While Paul's father is attempting to help his son successfully spend time away from home, he inadvertently communicates that this level of anxiety is warranted. Additionally, he communicates to Paul both that he is unable to calm himself without his father's presence and that it is appropriate to leave situations that create anxiety. While these are not the messages Paul's father intends to send, they are the ones Paul receives.

Negative Reinforcement

Fifteen-year-old Abby is old enough to obtain a learner's permit and begin to drive. However, she is adamant she is not going to do this because she "just knows" she will get into an accident and be hurt or hurt someone. Her parents listen to her concerns, calmly tell her this is unlikely, and promise they will be in the car with her as she learns to drive. When this doesn't assuage her anxiety, her parents become more direct. Her mother lectures her, saying, "This is ridiculous," demands that Abby study for half an hour each night, and proclaims she is "going to" take the test a week from Thursday and had "better not even think about trying to fail it." Every night Abby tearfully endures studying with her parents and is lectured on the childishness of her tears. After losing a screaming match about whether she will take the test, she reluctantly gets into the car and cries all the way to the examination office, where her parents admonish her that she had "better come out with a license." Abby passes her test, but her anxiety doesn't abate, and every time her parents want her to practice driving, a screaming match ensues, ending with Abby capitulating and crying while she white-knuckles her way through practice.

Abby's parents correctly identify that Abby's anxiety is based upon fears about events unlikely to occur and avoidance only feeds the fears. However, they do not validate Abby's fears or help her find ways to manage the emotions. This leaves Abby flooded with anxiety throughout the experience. In her brain, driving becomes wed with experiences of overwhelming anxiety. Every time she considers driving, her body recalls the intense anxiety she experienced while driving and begins to reexperience this anxiety, making it impossible for Abby to consider driving without feeling terrified.

Healthy Reinforcement

Parents often start by being overly responsive to their child's anxiety and, as their patience wanes and their frustration increases, move to more negative reinforcement. Both are entirely understandable; honestly, I have done (and occasionally still do) both with my own children. Understandable as they may be, neither are effective at anything other than reinforcing the avoidant behavior anxiety invites children into. Healthy reinforcement involves validating anxiety *and* reinforcing strategies they can or are using to manage the anxiety. I highlight the word *and* intentionally. *And* is not my normal reaction when my children are anxious. When I successfully validate my children's anxiety about doing something, I normally follow the validation with the word *but* rather than *and*. When validation is followed by *but*, it invalidates everything that was just said or done. "I know going to bed where it is dark is scary, *but* it's safe and you will be fine" is really saying "I know you are scared but you shouldn't be." This is problematic for children. It leaves them with two choices:

1. To hide or deny their feelings because their parents told them the feelings shouldn't be there.
2. To intensify the emotion to prove it is there, it is real, and it is justified.

Neither of these choices helps children learn to manage the emotion. Thus, it is important to validate emotions as real *and* help children engage in strategies to manage the emotions successfully. In this chapter we will integrate all the strategies learned in chapters 9 through 12 to help your child learn to manage their behavior. This process is a team effort requiring you and your child to work together.

Developing a Game Plan

By now, you and your child have consistently been spending special time together and have also been practicing skills to relax their body, manage anxious thoughts, and manage anxious feelings. We are going to put these skills together and begin to climb the Wall of Worry. Until now we have deliberately worked only with one or two items at the bottom of the wall to help your child become proficient at the skills we've been discussing. While we will continue working at the bottom of the wall for a bit, we want to paint a picture of getting to the top of the wall and conquering the fears up there too.

Step One: Develop a Vision

Take time with your child to talk about what it would be like to conquer the Wall of Worry and not be controlled or "bossed around" by those fears. As you have this conversation, remember your child may have no idea what their world would be like if it weren't controlled by fear. They may not remember a time in their life they weren't afraid. Have them dream about and talk about what it would be like if they weren't afraid about going out to recess, throwing up in the lunchroom, or being with people. One way to do this is to write a story together about a child who is afraid and conquers their fear. The story should describe all of the things the child can do after conquering the fear. This needs to be their story, not one you create for them. They may decide Sally's fear of getting picked on magically goes away and Sally is able to ask other kids to play and becomes the star soccer player. It doesn't matter if the story is unrealistic as long as your child begins seeing fear as conquerable. Older children might write a letter to themselves, cheering themselves on to victory over fear. Just like good cheerleaders see the team as capable of winning, in this letter your child should describe the ways they see themselves as capable of overcoming fear and doing what they wish or dream of doing. An example might look like this:

Dear Morgan,

God created you as a unique individual with a unique path to travel. The path has many forks and turns, and at each intersection you are faced with choices. I have seen you make so many intelligent and wise choices in so many areas of your life and am excited to see how you continue doing this moving forward.

When anxiety crept into your life, I watched it stealthily capture and imprison you within the small cell anxiety told you was safe. Anxiety imprisoned you but couldn't destroy the wonderful, intelligent, strong, creative, thoughtful, and persistent person you are.

You have begun learning about your captor and how to break free from the prison cell it confined you to, and I see the spark in your eye as you contemplate a prison break. As you practice the skills you are learning, the prison walls anxiety created are weakening. You may not see it just yet, but they are beginning to crumble! As the walls begin to crumble, there will be room for you to step out into freedom—freedom to hang out with friends, freedom to experiment with things you have longed to do, freedom to peacefully enjoy your day. You are an amazing young woman empowered by God to escape your captor and live free of anxiety. Keep going, because the prison walls of anxiety are breaking!

Regardless of how you and your child go about this, the goal is to develop a vision for life without the anxiety. For this to be successful, however, your child must want to overcome their anxiety. Some children don't see their anxiety as a problem. If this is the case, the two of you need to explore ways it is a problem. Aggie might not see roaring until everyone leaves him alone as a problem. However, is that really true? If Aggie roars every time someone comes close to his cage, how will he get food? People may leave Aggie alone when he roars, but won't that leave him alone in his cage with no one to do anything with? If Aggie roars every time the trainer comes into the cage, will he ever learn to do all the cool things his trainer wants to teach him?

Older children may think school avoidance isn't a problem, but is that really going to work for the rest of their life? They may avoid school and get a GED, but what will happen when they need to work, move into an apartment, or date? Without belittling your child, help them build a picture of why letting anxiety run their life isn't effective. Once they believe this, help them develop a picture of what it looks like to conquer anxiety.

After your child develops their picture of conquering anxiety, it's helpful for you to paint a picture that shows you believe they can accomplish this feat. Utilize the strategies for reinforcing a growth mindset from chapter 10 and create a picture of the internal qualities your child possesses that will enable them to conquer anxiety. You might say something like, "Since you were small, you have had an amazing ability to push through hard things and take on challenges. I have seen you use this to accomplish things that were hard—like when you wanted to ride a bike without training wheels. You wouldn't give up even when you fell the first few times. You pushed on and kept trying until you learned to do it. You are good at challenging yourself and then pushing yourself until you accomplish the challenge, and I think this will help you to conquer your anxiety."

Once you have created a vision, you may want to link success to something that matters to your child and is related to conquering the anxiety on the wall. We're wired to move away from painful experiences and toward pleasurable experiences. Climbing the Wall of Worry involves encountering painful feelings, so having something pleasurable for your child to work toward can be helpful. The reward must matter to your child and be linked to conquering the anxiety. If your child's greatest fear is sleeping in a room by themselves, using a trip to Disney World as a reward wouldn't fit well because it isn't linked to their types of fear. If their top fear on the Wall of Worry is sleeping alone in their room, a better reward might be getting to redecorate their room, choose a new paint color, and help paint their bedroom (provided this matters to them).

Step Two: Identify the First Step

It's time to begin the journey up the wall. You may want to draw a road up the wall with each of the fears as a stop on the road. At the top of the road is the desired outcome and/or reward. Be sure your child understands they won't be asked to climb the wall all at once, and each fear will be tackled in small increments. Have your child pick the first fear to tackle and explain that, together, you will be devising a "training plan" to conquer it. Talk about how Aggie's trainer might decide the first thing he is going to teach Aggie is how to sit in the back of his cage and not roar when the trainer comes in. Think together about things the lion trainer might do to teach Aggie to do this. Be sure your child understands the lion trainer wouldn't expect Aggie to just know how to sit without roaring when he enters the cage. You might talk about how the trainer could create a system so raw meat would fall in the back of the cage as he approaches the front of the cage. As Aggie gets the meat, he also learns to go to the back of the cage as the lion trainer approaches. After Aggie has learned this, the trainer might make the meat only fall when Aggie is in the back of the cage and doesn't roar. Once Aggie learns to go to the back of the cage without roaring as the lion trainer approaches the cage, the meat might only drop when Aggie stays in the back of the cage without roaring as the trainer opens the cage door slightly. The trainer would use this process until he can walk into the cage and stand there with Aggie sitting quietly in the back of the cage. Then, talk with your child about how the two of you will be devising a plan like this to climb the Wall of Worry, starting with the first fear.

If the first fear is being afraid to sleep alone, start where your child currently is and break this fear down into steps. If they currently go to bed with you and sleep in your bed every night, this is their starting point on the journey. Talk about the steps needed to arrive at the place where they are sleeping alone. The more your child can identify the steps, the better. They might create a list like this:

1. Go to bed in parents' room in their bed, with them in bed with me from the time I go to bed.
2. Go to bed in parents' room, and they sit beside the bed until I go to sleep and then come to bed later.
3. Go to bed in parents' room, and they read me a story and then leave after they put me to bed.
4. Go to bed in parents' room on the floor right beside their bed, and they read me a story and then leave after they put me to bed.
5. Go to bed on the floor in the hallway outside parents' room.

6. Go to bed in my bed, and my parents lie on the floor by the door until I go to sleep. I can come back and lie on the floor outside their door if I get scared in the night.

7. Go to bed in my bed, and my parents lie on the floor by the door until I go to sleep. If I wake up in the night, I will listen to a recording of my parents reading me a story until I go back to sleep.

8. Go to bed in my bed, and my parents lie on the floor by the door for ten minutes.

9. Go to bed in my bed, and my parents read me a story and then leave the room.

Your child may not generate all these steps, and it's okay if they don't. For some children, the best strategy is to just come up with the first step. If your child is currently only eating peanut butter sandwiches for fear of becoming sick, they might agree the first step is to stop watching you make the sandwich and trust you inspected the silverware before making the sandwich. They don't have to know other steps just yet if they see this step as something they are willing to conquer.

Step Three: Make a Training Plan

Just like Aggie's trainer needs a plan for what he will do to manage Aggie's roar, your child needs a concrete plan for how they will manage their body's sensations, thoughts, and feelings as they start learning the new behavior. Luckily, you have been practicing this along the way. Take the step you have just identified and talk through:

1. How they will calm their body when it becomes anxious as they attempt this activity.

2. Thoughts they anticipate having as they attempt this activity, and how they will address these thoughts.

3. Feelings they are likely to experience attempting this activity, the function of these feelings, and strategies to validate these feelings and calm them instead of fueling their flame.

Once the plan is made, rehearse it. Have your child imagine they are going to eat a peanut butter sandwich you made when they weren't present. Their body will start to feel tense, and they should use breathing and progressive relaxation to calm it. They will have thoughts like, *What if the knife wasn't clean and I get sick?* Help them to rehearse the facts they have previously identified when this occurs. They will feel fearful and can practice thanking their body for identifying a potential danger and review the ways they are safe. Have them rehearse the plan in their head until they can visualize themselves successfully overcoming all aspects of anxiety that arise. Older children may want to create a checklist of things they can do when they feel anxious. After they create the list, have them practice using this list as they visualize themselves successfully managing the anxiety associated with attempting the first step up their Wall of Worry.

Step Four: Implement the Training Plan

Pick a time when you and your child agree to put the plan in motion. Make sure this is a time when you won't be rushed and your child won't be overly tired or stressed by other things. For example, you might decide to implement the plan to go to sleep with parents sitting beside the bed instead of in bed on a Friday night so everyone can sleep in the next morning if needed. Remind your child of what they are working toward and how much this means to them. Reinforce that you believe in them and their ability to do hard things. Then put the plan in motion. When it is bedtime, have your child climb into bed and settle yourself into a chair. Read a bedtime story with them and then spend time praying with them using the safe-place prayer (chapter 7). When they have settled safely in the presence of Jesus, tell them goodnight and sit quietly. Your child may settle in and go right to sleep, or they may begin to become anxious. If that happens, have them rate how loud the anxiety is roaring at them using the SUD (chapter 9). If their SUD is above a five, ask them what they can do to lower this number. You want to be a cheerleader and a coach—not the one telling them what to do. If they have a checklist, have them practice the first item on the list slowly and deliberately and then pay attention to how this impacts their SUD. They can repeat the activity or go to the next item on the list depending on what is creating the anxiety. If they find their body tenses up as they think about going to sleep and having their parents leave, they may need to do the progressive relaxation exercise. However, if their mind is filled with "what if" thoughts, start with some good detective work. Use the strategies previously identified until they quiet the "roar" to a place where it feels manageable even if it isn't totally gone.

Cheerlead by focusing on strengths you see as your child works to use their new skills. Things like bravery, perseverance, and creative problem solving reinforce a growth mindset for your child while also encouraging them to continue working to do difficult things. The younger your child is, the more actively involved you will need to be. However, don't overfunction for your child by doing things they can do for themselves. If they are emotionally flooded, you may need to provide verbal prompts to help them, as they will struggle to think clearly. If the thought of you leaving rather than staying in the room all night creates intense fear, you might suggest the two of you breathe together for a few minutes to help both of you relax. You can count for the first couple of breaths and then have your child count for the next few. Gradually hand responsibility back to your child. The goal is for them to manage the anxiety rather than avoiding it or white-knuckling through. Help your child identify the skills they can use and successfully implement those skills. This is going to take time—and a lot of patience on your part! Eventually, your child will fall asleep and you should get up and leave the room. Twenty minutes later, your child may be awake and screaming for you. Repeat the process you previously went through until your child is asleep, then leave once more. You may have to repeat the process multiple times the first night. The goal is for your child to be asleep when you finally come to bed and to have slept for at least a brief time without you in the room. If this happens, you have been successful, and you will want to celebrate this success in the morning.

Step Five: Celebrate and Reinforce Success

Celebration and reinforcement of even the smallest positive steps are a critical part of helping your child learn to manage anxiety. Reinforce the positive things your child does and talk through how they accomplished each one. Statements like, "I was so impressed by how you got your body to relax when you woke up and I wasn't there. How did you do that?" give your child a chance to review what they did and to "brag" about how skillfully they navigated the challenge. Celebrating that your child used spaghetti and noodle arms to relax may seem trivial when you still have a five-year-old sleeping with you, but it bolsters their confidence and links positive feelings to this new behavior. Your goal is to reinforce the ways your child skillfully works to manage anxiety while simultaneously not inadvertently reinforcing avoidant behaviors.

Step Six: Plan Repetition

It can be tempting to skip this step, but that is unwise. Long-term success requires practicing each step until your child can do it while keeping their SUD under five the entire time. If you move forward prematurely, the anxiety produced by moving forward will augment the anxiety they are already experiencing and will likely be more than they can tolerate and still effectively utilize their skills. If Lamar practiced going to sleep with you sitting in a chair next to him on Friday night, don't wait until Monday night to try again, as this allows two days of utilizing old coping skills prior to practicing the new skills again. Consecutive practice days strengthen new skills and extinguish the reflex of old skills. Your child will probably want to avoid trying again, and it may be tempting to give in, so remind yourself it takes consecutive days of practice to develop new behaviors!

Step Seven: Move to the Next Step

When your child has successfully kept their SUD below five for several repetitions of the same activity, and this success has been celebrated, it is time to move to the next step. If your child has learned to go to sleep with you sitting in a chair beside them, it is now time to plan for leaving the room after reading them a story and praying with them. Repeat the same process until your child is successfully sleeping in their own room. When this occurs, celebrate wildly! If you agreed your child could redecorate their room when this occurred, don't put this activity off. You want them to connect their hard work with the reward. Additionally, find a way to mark their progress on the Wall of Worry. Your child might use a picture of themselves to mark their progress up the wall. Making sure they show their progress in meaningful ways is extremely important.

Some steps up the wall may take little time while others seem insurmountable. Some steps may be conquered before you get to them because your child will begin to generalize the skills they have been practicing and use them in new situations without thinking about it. If this happens, celebrate the step even though it is out of order. As you move along the wall, rehearse what will be true when your child successfully arrives at the top and conquers their fears.

Obstacles and Stalls

It is not unusual for children to experience new fears they will need to add to their Wall of Worry. This can create negative emotions for you and your child unless you see it as a normal part of the process. Anxiety tends to move from one thing to another before it is successfully managed. Your child may go from worrying about throwing up in class to obsessing about answering a question wrong. Both worries center around fear of what others will think, so it makes sense the circumstances will vary until the underlying fear has been mastered. When worries appear to "jump," look for the underlying theme and identify ways your child can challenge this fear.

Some children make a plan but stall out when it's time to implement this plan. This happens if the steps involved are too big, if the skills needed haven't been sufficiently practiced, or if the child isn't truly invested in learning to manage anxiety. If your child stalls out when attempting to implement their plan, try making the first step smaller. If your child accomplishes part of the plan but becomes overwhelmed with anxiety and can't use skills to lower their anxiety level, identify the skills they are struggling with. If fearful thinking keeps getting in the way, go back and practice the skill of managing thinking patterns until they can consistently challenge their "what if" thoughts. Then attempt to implement the plan again. If your child appears to have the skills yet refuses to implement the plan, they may not see the pain of learning to manage anxiety as worth what they gain in the end. You cannot force your child to be ready to change. If your child falls into this category, professional assistance from a therapist may help determine how to overcome this obstacle.

≡ Applying What You Learned

Anxiety is created by different factors, and when a child feels anxious, the experience is overwhelming. Learning to utilize all the skills we have talked about requires incredible bravery, extensive practice, and a lot of cheerleading from parents.

1. As you discussed the strategies in this chapter with your child, what was most appealing to them? How can you capitalize on this as you work to implement the strategies outlined?

2. As you read the chapter, which parts of making and implementing a plan to manage anxiety seemed most overwhelming and daunting for you? Which parts concerned your child the most? How can you address what seems overwhelming or daunting to each of you? What resources would be helpful?

3. Construct a plan with your child to begin implementing the strategies outlined in this chapter. As always, approach this as a team effort!

Helping your child learn to successfully manage anxiety while engaging in anxiety-provoking activities is difficult and time-consuming. You may find yourself trying the steps outlined in this chapter, then giving up and allowing old coping strategies to seep back in. Trust me—it happens a lot! If you find this happening, avoid self-condemnation or throwing in the towel. Instead, simply start again. These strategies require you to learn new skills just as your child has to learn new skills. It is difficult, so be patient with yourself and be patient with your child.

FOURTEEN

Moving Forward

I love to learn, and one of my favorite parts of my job is attending conferences and classes full of new therapy strategies. After returning from one such conference, I sat down for supper with my middle school–aged children and began catching up on the events that had transpired in their lives while I was gone. At some point in the conversation, one of them quipped, "So, what new thing are we going to have to put up with as you try to make us better—until you forget about it?" Ouch! I wanted them to be wrong. But I typically came back from conferences laden with new parenting techniques I vowed to implement. For the first few weeks I would be consistent and committed, and things moved in a new direction. However, my children were right . . . things eventually drifted back to "normal" as the new strategies fell to the wayside. Why did all of those well-intended attempts fail? Simply put, change is hard!

It's hard, but it's not impossible. Your child can make changes in their life that decrease worry and anxiety. However, it won't happen simply by reading this book or because you and your child have enough willpower. Neither of those things has the power to produce lasting change.

Why Is Change So Hard?

Early in my career, I worked with patients in kidney failure. For these patients to remain healthy, even with dialysis, they had to make significant changes to their diet and water intake. No matter how clearly they were told that failing to make these changes would result in potential death, the vast majority struggled to change. My experience is supported by studies of heart bypass patients that show only 9 percent of them make the lifestyle changes recommended by their doctor to avoid potential death.[1] As medical institutions attempt to provide better treatment, studying why this occurs is important. What is emerging is a deeper understanding of how behavior patterns form and what is required for change.

God designed the human brain with enormous potential for change *and* a predisposition to keep everything the same. The brain forms neural pathways much like a path is created through the jungle. The first time through the jungle is incredibly difficult and takes immense focus, energy, and work as you pick your way through, chop down everything standing in your way, and ward off creatures attempting to thwart your efforts. However, going down the same path the next day will be significantly easier, and if you travel the same path every day for a month, it will become well-worn, with each trip requiring less exertion. Eventually, taking this path will be the preferable thing to do—even if it doesn't lead you exactly where you want to go.

When we learn to perform an activity like writing our name, neurons in our brain send signals to one another that keep our eyes focused and create the appropriate hand motions. Initially, this takes considerable thought, concentration, and effort. However, as we continue to practice, these neurons begin to fire more rapidly and smoothly while requiring less effort to do so. As Donald Hebb described in 1949, neurons that fire together wire themselves together,[2] allowing our brain to efficiently and effectively complete millions of complex tasks while expending minimal energy. These habits and routines are controlled by the *basal ganglia*, within what is sometimes referred to as the *reptilian brain*. This part of the brain utilizes little energy and doesn't change easily. When we repeat actions or thought patterns, we strengthen the basal ganglia neural connections around this activity.

Simultaneously, neurons are also forming new connections that change what we think, feel, and do. This process, called *neuroplasticity*, gives humans immense potential for change. Changing habits or thought patterns requires building new pathways, which entails conscious thought—something that occurs primarily within the brain's prefrontal cortex. While the basal ganglia operate like a fuel-efficient car on a freeway with the cruise control engaged, the prefrontal cortex functions more like an ATV attempting to navigate through the jungle. Building new neural pathways is energy intense, requires deliberate and focused attention, and is emotionally uncomfortable or even painful. People override this discomfort and press on to try something new when it is unique and/or their stress level is low. It is more difficult to cope with the required expenditure of energy and emotional discomfort when the new wears off and/or there are more stressors. When we are stressed, tired, or distracted, our basal ganglia kick in and we do what we have always done, even if it's not what we want to do.

Children struggling with anxiety have an additional factor complicating things further. God designed the human brain to keep us safe, which means it takes in copious data, compares it to similar situations from the past, and correlates it with what is expected to happen in order to detect anomalies that might signal danger. If an anomaly is detected, the amygdala begins draining energy from the prefrontal cortex to mobilize the fight-flight-freeze response. This process is supercharged for children struggling with anxiety, making their bodies move to fight-flight-freeze in circumstances where no danger exists. Even the thought of leaving the house can send the brain into fight-flight-freeze for a child struggling with agoraphobia.

Reading this may make you wonder, Why bother trying? While these factors are at play, understanding them and working with them instead of assuming they don't exist will allow you and your child to successfully implement what you have learned. Let's look at how you could do this.

Pleasure versus Pain

Change feels threatening, and we often attempt to threaten ourselves or others into change. This works directly against the brain's desire to minimize threats and maximize pleasure. Our autonomic response system is well honed to flee from threats, and the prefrontal cortex must actively convince us to approach possible rewards until we experience pleasure from the new activity. Once the pleasure has been experienced, the brain is highly motivated to experience it again.

For example, if your child struggles with agoraphobia and tells themselves, *Stop being such a fraidy cat and just go get in the car and go to church like normal people do*, your child is threatening themselves with being abnormal. Additionally, their amygdala is draining energy from their prefrontal cortex because it fears something bad will happen if they leave the house, creating panic that causes them to breathe faster, sweat, experience nausea, and shake. This is incredibly painful physically and emotionally, so your child's brain is highly motivated to do whatever it takes to make the feelings *stop*. The only positive thing to move toward is the comfort of the living room, so this is likely what will happen. The moment your child decides not to leave the house, their brain begins to calm and they feel better (more pleasure than they were feeling before), which reinforces staying home as better than leaving.

On the flip side, if sixteen-year-old Amanda fears speaking in public, she will experience a great deal of distress as she prepares for a school presentation. However, if she successfully completes the presentation, her peers tell her how much they enjoyed it, and she gets a good grade, her brain will release dopamine, which is pleasurable, and she will be motivated to do things that will re-create this release of dopamine.

The neuropathways telling your child to avoid speaking in public or leaving the house are much like the Mississippi River. Changing the path of the Mississippi would be difficult, especially if you can't stop the water while attempting to do it. The same is true of attempting to change existing neural pathways. Building new neural pathways is easier than changing existing pathways and, as you build new pathways, it naturally weakens the old ones.[3]

To build new neural pathways, set goals with your child about what you are each *going* to do rather than what you need to *stop* doing. Scripture contains more things we are supposed to do than things we aren't supposed to do. God designed us to be more motivated to experience pleasure—particularly the pleasure of his presence—than to avoid pain. Understanding God loves and delights in us causes us to want to move toward him, while knowing he wants us to stop sinning causes us to want to hide from him. "I will grow to the place I can go to the movies with my friends," for example, gives your child something positive to work toward. Take a minute now to think about a positive goal *you* want to work toward as a result of the things you read in this book.

Different Levels of Readiness for Change

While you may be ready for your child to conquer their anxiety, they may believe their anxiety is necessary and see no reason to change a thing. It is important to accurately assess where you are and where your child is. Sometimes, children desperately want change, but the time and effort required on the part of their parents feels overwhelming given everything else going on for them as an individual, parent, spouse, and/or employee. Other times, parents are fed up with their child's anxiety, but the child sees absolutely nothing wrong and believes if others would simply comply with their requests everything would be fine. When two people aren't at the same stage of change, no matter their age or relationship, it is important to remember you control yourself but are not able to control others.

While you can't control others, relationships are like a good waltz. If one partner in the waltz changes what they are doing, it changes the dance. Initially, there may be toes stepped on and the dance may look clumsy and painful. The fact one partner moves differently means the other partner can't continue doing things as they have always done them. They will do one of two things:

1. *Up the ante.* If the partner is invested in the old way of doing things, they may more forcefully engage in the old pattern, hoping this will cause the partner who changed things to go back to the old familiar steps. If you begin changing some of your behaviors that were inadvertently reinforcing your child's anxiety, your child may become more demanding and emotional in an attempt to get you to revert back to old behaviors. Resist this urge and just firmly keep doing things the new way.

2. *Gradually conform.* While initially startled by the new dance movement, some partners gradually adjust to the new pattern. This sometimes occurs after upping the ante and finding their partner is unwilling to revert back to old behaviors, or it may just naturally happen—especially if the partner sees purpose and meaning in learning to do things differently.

If you and your child don't have the same readiness for change, enlisting the assistance of a counselor can be useful. It is helpful to have someone work with you and your child to increase awareness of ways each of you can move differently in the relationship dance to better manage your child's anxiety.

In Conclusion

This book will only be useful if its contents are put into practice. Some children will learn skills to effectively manage the anxiety they are currently experiencing, and it won't be an issue in their life moving forward. For other children, learning to manage anxiety will be an ongoing process that won't be fully completed until the day they stand before God in their perfected state. Either way, it is essential to graciously examine where you and your child are and set goals to begin moving forward. Embracing the journey of learning to manage anxiety is part of becoming everything God created you and your child to be and is worth the time and energy needed.

I pray you and your child experience his love and his encouragement as you journey with him.

Attachment Style Inventory

Circle each of the statements below that fit you.

1. I often worry the people I am closest to will stop loving me.
2. I fear once someone gets to know the real me, they won't like who I am.
3. When I don't have deep, emotionally connected relationships in my life, I feel anxious and incomplete.
4. When someone I am close to is distant or unavailable, I find myself fearful they may find someone else they would rather be close to.
5. When I express my feelings to the people I am closest to, I am fearful they will not feel the same about me.
6. I think about the people I am close to a lot.
7. I tend to quickly become close and emotionally connected to people.
8. I am sensitive to the moods of the people I am close to.
9. I worry that if the people I am close to leave, I will have difficulty finding others to be close to.

10. If someone I've been close to begins to act cold and distant, I worry I've done something wrong.

11. I tend to avoid telling someone I am close to that I am upset, because I don't want to damage the relationship.

12. I find it easy to be affectionate with people I am close to.

13. I feel comfortable depending on people I am close to.

14. I am generally satisifed with my close relationships.

15. I have little difficulty expressing my needs and wants to people I am close to.

16. I can easily be emotionally present with people and empathically connect to where they are at emotionally when they are upset.

17. I am not easily threatened by the strengths of the people around me.

18. I believe most people are essentially honest and dependable.

19. I am comfortable sharing my personal thoughts and feelings with the people I am close to.

20. An argument with people I am close to doesn't usually cause me to question our relationship.

21. Sometimes people see me as boring because I don't create much drama in relationships.

22. When I disagree with someone, I feel comfortable expressing my opinions.

23. If someone I'm close to begins to act cold and distant, I may wonder what's happening, but I am relatively sure it is probably not about me or they will tell me if it is.

24. I find I bounce back quickly after someone leaves my life. I can easily put someone who has left my life out of my mind.

25. I find it difficult to be emotionally present with people and to match their emotions when they are feeling upset.

26. My independence is a high value.

27. I prefer not to share my innermost feelings with the people I am close to.

28. I find it difficult to depend on people.

29. I sometimes feel angry or annoyed with people I am close to when we are having deep conversations that contain intense emotions.

30. It makes me nervous when people get close to me emotionally.

31. During conflict, I can get to the place where I express emotions in ways that cause others to distance from me either emotionally or physically.

32. The people I am close to often want me to be more emotionally vulnerable than I am comfortable with.

33. When someone likes me, I find myself initially interested but rapidly lose interest in the relationship.

34. I don't like feeling that people are dependent on me.

35. If someone I've been close to begins to act cold and distant, I find myself feeling somewhat indifferent about this.

Total number of circles on 1–11: _____
Preoccupied Attachment

Total number of circles on 12–23: _____
Stable Attachment

Total number of circles on 24–35: _____
Avoidant Attachment

If you find your numbers evenly spread between preoccupied and avoidant, this would suggest you might have a fearful attachment style.[1]

Growth Mindset Resources

Books for Elementary-Aged Children

Peyton Curley, *Growth Mindset Workbook for Kids: 55 Fun Activities to Think Creatively, Solve Problems, and Love Learning* (Emeryville, CA: Rockridge Press, 2020)

Ginny Kochis, *Made for Greatness: A Growth Mindset Journal for Courageous Catholic Youth* (Springville, UT: Vervante, 2019)

Brandy Thompson, *Learn, Grow, Succeed!: A Kids Growth Mindset Journal* (Emeryville, CA: Rockridge Press, 2019)

Books for Adolescents

Caren Baruch-Feldman, *The Grit Guide for Teens: A Workbook to Help You Build Perseverance, Self-Control, and a Growth Mindset* (Oakland, CA: Instant Help Books, 2017)

Pretty Pickles, *Growth Mindset Journal for Teen and Tween Boys: Hey Dude, You've Got This* (independently published, 2020)

Iona Yeung, *Growth Mindset Journal for Teen and Tween Girls* (independently published, 2019)

Books for Adults

Carol Dweck, *Mindset: The New Psychology of Success*, updated ed. (New York: Ballantine, 2016)

Joshua Moore and Helen Glasgow, *The Growth Mindset: A Guide to Professional and Personal Growth*, The Art of Growth, vol. 1 (Scotts Valley, CA: CreateSpace, 2017)

Mary Cay Ricci, *Mindsets for Parents: Strategies to Encourage Growth Mindsets in Kids* (Waco, TX: Prufrock Press, 2016)

Feeling Words

Anger and Resentment

Agitated	Enraged	Miffed
Angry	Furious	Resentful
Annoyed	Galled	Seething
Bitter	Had it	Ticked
Bristle	Hateful	Upset
Bugged	Impatient	Uptight
Chagrined	Indignant	Vengeful
Disgusted	Infuriated	Violent
Dismayed	Livid	

Anxiety and Tension

Afraid	Apprehensive	Defensive
Alarmed	Awkward	Desperate
Anxious	Bashful	Distrustful

Dread	Nervous	Terrified
Embarrassed	Panicky	Terror-stricken
Fearful	Paralyzed	Threatened
Fidgety	Rattled	Timid
Frantic	Restless	Uneasy
Frightened	Scared	Unsure
Hesitant	Shaken	Uptight
Horrified	Shocked	Vulnerable
Intimidated	Shy	Worried
Jittery	Stunned	
Jumpy	Tense	

Caring and Loving

Accept	Devoted	Prize
Admire	Enamored	Regard
Adore	Esteem	Respect
Affectionate	Fond	Tender
Attached	Friendly	Trust
Care	Idolize	Value
Cherish	Infatuated	Warm
Close	Like	Worship
Concerned	Love	
Dear	Positive	

Competence and Strength

Able	Capable	Confident
Adequate	Committed	Convicted
Brave	Competent	Courageous

Daring	Inspired	Sharp
Determined	Mastery	Skillful
Effective	Potent	Strong
Firm	Powerful	Successful
Forceful	Ready	Sure
Important	Resolute	Trusting
Impressive	Secure	Well-equipped
Influential	Self-reliant	

Confusion and Troubled

Adrift	Disorganized	Stumped
Ambivalent	Disturbed	Torn
Baffled	Floored	Trapped
Befuddled	Flustered	Troubled
Bewildered	Frustrated	Uncertain
Bothered	Lost	Uncomfortable
Conflicted	Mixed-up	Undecided
Confounded	Overwhelmed	Uneasy
Confused	Perplexed	Unsure
Disconcerted	Puzzled	

Depression and Discouragement

Anguished	Deflated	Disheartened
Awful	Dejected	Dismal
Bad	Demoralized	Distressed
Blah	Depressed	Down
Bleak	Despondent	Downcast
Blue	Disappointed	Dreadful
Brokenhearted	Discouraged	Forlorn

Gloomy	Lousy	Sorrowful
Grieved	Low	Tearful
Grim	Melancholy	Terrible
Hopeless	Miserable	Unhappy
Horrible	Pessimistic	Weepy
Kaput	Rotten	
Lost	Sad	

Guilt and Embarrassment

Ashamed	Foolish	Remorseful
Branded	Goofed	Responsible
Crummy	Guilty	Ridiculous
Degraded	Horrible	Rotten
Demeaned	Humiliated	Silly
Disgraced	In error	Stupid
Embarrassed	Lament	Unforgivable
Exposed	Mortified	Wrong
Faulty	Regretful	

Happiness and Satisfaction

Calm	Excited	Happy
Cheerful	Fantastic	Hopeful
Content	Fine	Jolly
Delighted	Fulfilled	Joyful
Ecstatic	Glad	Jubilant
Elated	Glowing	Lighthearted
Elevated	Good	Marvelous
Enthusiastic	Gratified	Mellow
Euphoric	Great	Pleased

Satisfied	Super	Thrilled
Serene	Superb	Tranquil
Splendid	Terrific	Wonderful

Inadequacy and Helplessness

Awkward	Incapable	Puny
Clumsy	Incompetent	Small
Crippled	Incomplete	Stupid
Defeated	Ineffective	Unable
Deficient	Inefficient	Uncertain
Emasculated	Inept	Unfit
Finished	Inferior	Unimportant
Helpless	Inhibited	Useless
Immobilized	Insecure	Weak
Impaired	Insignificant	Whipped
Impotent	Lacking	Worthless
Inadequate	Overwhelmed	

Loneliness

Abandoned	Distant	Left out
Alienated	Estranged	Lonely
Alone	Excluded	Lonesome
Aloof	Forlorn	Rejected
Apart	Forsaken	Remote
Cut off	Isolated	Shut out

Rejection and Offensiveness

| Abused | Betrayed | Criticized |
| Belittled | Cheapened | Crushed |

Debased	Exploited	Rejected
Degraded	Hurt	Ridiculed
Depreciated	Impugned	Ruined
Destroyed	Maligned	Scored
Devalued	Minimized	Slandered
Devastated	Mistreated	Slighted
Disappointed	Mocked	Tortured
Discarded	Neglected	Unappreciated
Discounted	Offended	Underestimated
Discredited	Overlooked	Used
Disparaged	Pained	Wounded

Feeling Faces

Positive Emotions

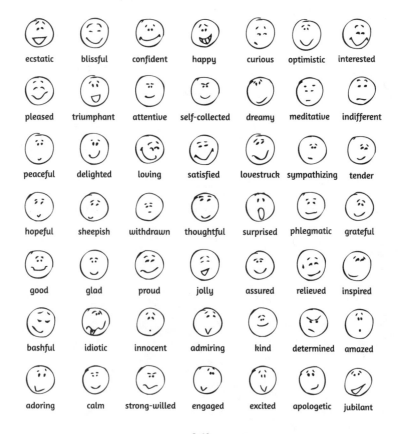

Negative Emotions

demure	cautious	guilty	frightened	unhappy	regretful	sad
envious	unsure	disappointed	hurt	bored	annoyed	shy
insulted	sneaky	discontented	ashamed	wistful	suffering	repentant
nervous	humiliated	weak	astonished	jealous	obstinate	grieving
enraged	speechless	depressed	upset	lonely	negative	resentful
arrogant	anxious	aggressive	eavesdropping	hopeless	cynical	mean
gloomy	heart-broken	contemptuous	impatient	prudish	suspicious	shocked

Notes

Chapter 1 Why Children Don't Act and React like Adults

1. Kathleen Stassen Berger, *The Developing Person through Childhood and Adolescence*, 10th ed. (New York: Worth, 2015), 176.

2. Stassen Berger, *Developing Person*, 184–85.

3. Jaak Panksepp and Douglas Watt, "What Is Basic about Basic Emotions? Lasting Lessons from Affective Neuroscience," *Emotion Review* 3, no. 4 (2011): 387–96.

4. Melvin Konner, "Evolutionary Foundations of Cultural Psychology," in *Handbook of Cultural Psychology*, ed. Shinobu Kitayama and Dov Cohen (New York: Guilford Press, 2007), 77–105.

5. Carroll E. Izard, "Emotion Theory and Research: Highlights, Unanswered Questions, and Merging Issues," *Annual Review of Psychology* 60 (2009): 1–25.

6. Stassen Berger, *Developing Person*, 205.

7. Stassen Berger, *Developing Person*, 245.

8. Timothy J. Silk and Amanda G. Wood, "Lessons about Neurodevelopment from Anatomical Magnetic Resonance Imaging," *Journal of Developmental and Behavioral Pediatrics* 32, no. 2 (2011): 158–68.

9. Rima Hanania, "Two Types of Perseveration in the Dimension Change Card Sort Task," *Journal of Experimental Child Psychology* 107, no. 3 (2010): 325–36.

10. Stassen Berger, *Developing Person*, 293.

11. Stassen Berger, *Developing Person*, 278.

12. Alison Gopnik, "Theories, Language, and Culture: Whorf without Wincing," in *Language Acquisition and Conceptual Development*, ed. Melissa Bowerman and Stephen Levinson (New York: Cambridge University Press, 2001), 61.

13. Katya Rubia et al., "Progressive Increase of Frontostriatal Brain Activation from Childhood to Adulthood During Event-Related Tasks of Cognitive Control," *Human Brain Mapping* 27, no. 12 (2006): 973–93.

14. Stassen Berger, *Developing Person*, 251.

15. Kevin S. LaBar, "Beyond Fear: Emotional Memory Mechanisms in the Human Brain," *Current Directions in Psychological Science* 16, no. 4 (2007): 173–77.

16. Frank W. Paulus et al., "Anxiety Disorders and Behavioral Inhibition in Preschool Children: A Population-Based Study," *Child Psychiatry and Human Development* 46, no. 1 (2014): 150–57.

17. Peter Stern, "Connection, Connection, Connection . . .," *Science* 342, no. 6158 (2013): 577.

18. Carter Wendelken et al., "Neural Indices of Improved Attentional Modulation Over Middle Childhood," *Developmental Cognitive Neuroscience* 1, no. 2 (2011): 175–86.

19. Michael S. C. Thomas et al., "The Development of Metaphorical Language Comprehension in Typical Development and in Williams Syndrome," *Journal of Experimental Child Psychology* 106, no. 2–3 (2010): 99–114.

20. Stassen Berger, *Developing Person*, 384.

21. Spencer A. Rathus, *Childhood and Adolescence: Voyages in Development*, 4th ed. (Belmont, CA: Wadsworth Cengage Learning, 2011), 376.

22. Stassen Berger, *Developing Person*, 411.

23. Rathus, *Childhood and Adolescence*, 410.

24. Pamela Davis-Kean, Justin Jager, and Willard Andrew Collins, "The Self in Action: An Emerging Link between Self-Beliefs and Behaviors in Middle Childhood," *Child Development Perspectives* 3, no. 3 (2009): 184–88.

25. Lan Nguyen Chaplin and Deborah Roedder John, "Growing Up in a Material World: Age Differences in Materialism in Children and Adolescents," *Journal of Consumer Research* 34, no. 4 (2007): 480–93.

26. Stassen Berger, *Developing Person*, 415.

27. Daniel G. Whitney and Mark D. Peterson, "US National and State-Level Prevalence of Mental Health Disorders and Disparities of Mental Health Care Use in Children," *Journal of American Medical Association Pediatric* 173, no. 4 (2019): 389–91.

28. "Mental Health Myths and Facts," MentalHealth.gov, August 29, 2017, https://www.mentalhealth.gov/basics/mental-health-myths-facts.

29. Rathus, *Childhood and Adolescence*, 446.

30. Beatriz Luna et al., "The Teenage Brain: Cognitive Control and Motivation," *Current Directions in Psychological Science* 22, no. 2 (2013): 94–100.

31. Lyn Turkstra, Angela Ciccia, and Christine Seaton, "Interactive Behaviors in Adolescent Conversation Dyads," *Language, Speech, and Hearing Services in Schools* 34, no. 2 (2003): 117–27.

32. Stassen Berger, *Developing Person*, 477.

33. Catherine Sebastian, Stephanie Burnett, and Sarah-Jayne Blakemore, "Development of the Self-Concept During Adolescence," *Trends in Cognitive Sciences* 12, no. 11 (2008): 441–46.

34. Adriana Galván, "The Teenage Brain: Sensitivity to Rewards," *Current Directions in Psychological Science* 22, no. 2 (2013): 88–93.

35. Dustin Albert, Jason Chein, and Laurence Steinberg, "The Teenage Brain: Peer Influences on Adolescent Decision Making," *Current Directions in Psychological Science* 22, no. 2 (2013): 114–20.

36. Zoe A. Klein and Russell D. Romeo, "Changes in Hypothalamic—Pituitary—Adrenal Stress Responsiveness Before and After Puberty in Rats," *Hormones and Behavior* 64, no. 2 (2013): 357–63.

37. Janne Vanhalst et al., "Low Self-Esteem as a Risk Factor for Loneliness in Adolescence: Perceived—but Not Actual—Social Acceptance as an Underlying Mechanism," *Journal of Abnormal Child Psychology* 41, no. 7 (2013): 1067–81.

38. Stassen Berger, *Developing Person*, 518.

39. Kathryn M. LaFontana and Antonius H. N. Cillessen, "Developmental Changes in the Priority of Perceived Status in Childhood and Adolescence," *Social Development* 19, no. 1 (2010): 130–47.

40. Ronald C. Kessler et al., "Prevalence, Persistence, and Sociodemographic Correlates of DSM-IV Disorders in the National Comorbidity Survey Replication Adolescent Supplement," *Archives of General Psychiatry* 69, no. 4 (2012): 372–80.

41. Arialdi M. Miniño, "Mortality among Teenagers Ages 12–19 Years: United States, 1999–2006," Centers for Disease Control and Prevention, November 6, 2015, https://www.cdc.gov/nchs/products/databriefs/db37.htm.

42. Rubina Kapil, "5 Surprising Mental Health Statistics," Mental Health First Aid USA, February 6, 2019, https://www.mentalhealthfirstaid.org/2019/02/5-surprising-mental-health-statistics/.

Chapter 2 Normal Childhood Development or Anxiety?

1. Aditi Nerurkar et al., "When Physicians Counsel about Stress: Results of a National Study," *Journal of American Medical Association Internal Medicine* 173, no. 1 (2013): 76–77.

2. Reem M. Ghandour et al., "Prevalence and Treatment of Depression, Anxiety, and Conduct Problems in U.S. Children," *Journal of Pediatrics* 206 (March 2019): 258.

3. Rebecca H. Bitsko et al., "Epidemiology and Impact of Healthcare Provider Diagnosed Anxiety and Depression among US Children," *Journal of Developmental and Behavioral Pediatrics* 39, no. 5 (2018): 395–403.

4. Ghandour et al., "Prevalence and Treatment," 256–67.

5. American Psychiatric Association, *Diagnostic and Statistical Manual of Mental Disorders*, 5th ed. (DSM-5) (Arlington: American Psychiatric Association, 2013), 190–91.

6. DSM-5, 202–3.

7. DSM-5, 195.

8. DSM-5, 197–98.

9. DSM-5, 237–38.

10. DSM-5, 217–18.

11. DSM-5, 280–81.

12. DSM-5, 271–74.

13. DSM-5, 208–9.

14. DSM-5, 222.

Chapter 3 Helping Children Understand They Are Not Their Anxiety

1. "2010 Stress in America Report," American Psychological Association, November 9, 2010, https://www.apa.org/news/press/releases/stress/2010/national-report.pdf.

2. "About Social Determinants of Health (SDOH)," Centers for Disease Control and Prevention, accessed September 22, 2021, https://www.cdc.gov/social determinants/about.html.

3. Barna Group, *The Connected Generation: How Christian Leaders Around the World Can Strengthen Faith and Well-Being Among 18–35-Year-Olds* (Ventura, CA: Barna Group, 2019), 18–55.

4. Barry R. Chiswick and Donka M. Mirtcheva, "Religion and Child Health," *IZA Discussion Paper*, no. 5215 (September 2010).

5. Beth Azar, "A Reason to Believe," *Monitor on Psychology* 41, no. 11 (2010): 52.

Chapter 4 Biology Affects Anxiety

1. Hae-Ran Na et al., "The Genetic Basis of Panic Disorder," *Journal of Korean Medical Science* 26, no. 6 (2011): 701–10.

2. Lakshmi N. Ravindran and Murray B. Stein, "The Pharmacologic Treatment of Anxiety Disorders: A Review of Progress," *Journal of Clinical Psychiatry* 71, no. 7 (2010): 839–54.

3. Gregor Hasler et al., "Effect of Acute Psychological Stress on Prefrontal GABA Concentration Determined by Proton Magnetic Resonance Spectroscopy," *American Journal of Psychiatry* 167, no. 10 (2010): 1226–31.

4. Remmelt R. Shür et al., "Brain GABA Levels Across Psychiatric Disorders: A Systematic Literature Review and Meta-Analysis of H-MRS Studies," *Human Brain Mapping* 37, no. 9 (2016): 337–52.

5. Uwe Rudolph and Frédéric Knoflach, "Beyond Classical Benzodiazepines: Novel Therapeutic Potential of GABAA Receptor Subtypes," *Nature Reviews Drug Discovery* 10, no. 9 (2011): 685–97.

6. Michael Liebrenz et al., "High-Dose Benzodiazepine Dependence: A Qualitative Study of Patients' Perception on Cessation and Withdrawal," *Boston Medical Center Psychiatry* 15, no. 116 (2015): https://doi.org/10.1186/s12888 -015-0493-y.

7. Joshua P. Smith and Sarah W. Book, "Anxiety and Substance Use Disorders: A Review," *Psychiatric Times* 25, no. 10 (2008): 19.

8. "Why You Should Talk With Your Child about Alcohol and Other Drugs," Substance Abuse and Mental Health Services Administration, April 22, 2020, https://www.samhsa.gov/underage-drinking/parent-resources/why-you-should -talk-your-child.

9. Matt G. Kushner et al., "Epidemiological Perspectives on Co-Occurring Anxiety Disorder and Substance Use Disorder," in *Anxiety and Substance Use Disorders: The Vicious Cycle of Comorbidity*, ed. Sherry H. Stewart and Patricia J. Conrod (New York: Springer, 2008), 3–17.

10. Steven E. Bruce et al., "Influence of Psychiatric Comorbidity on Recovery and Recurrence in Generalized Anxiety Disorder, Social Phobia, and Panic Disorder: A 12-Year Prospective Study," *American Journal of Psychiatry* 162, no. 6 (2005): 1179–87.

11. Michael H. Bonnet et al., "The Use of Stimulants to Modify Performance during Sleep Loss: A Review by the Sleep Deprivation and Stimulant Task Force of the American Academy of Sleep Medicine," *Sleep* 28, no. 9 (2005): 1163–87.

12. Amy M. Branum, Lauren M. Rossen, and Kenneth C. Schoendorf, "Trends in Caffeine Intake among US Children and Adolescents," *Pediatrics* 133, no. 3 (2014): 386–93.

13. Malcolm Bruce et al., "Anxiogenic Effects of Caffeine in Patients with Anxiety Disorders," *Archives of General Psychiatry* 49, no. 11 (1992): 867–69.

14. Michelle Murphy and Julian G. Mercer, "Diet-Regulated Anxiety," *International Journal of Endocrinology* (August 20, 2013): https://doi.org/10.1155/2013/701967.

15. Karen M. Davison and Bonnie J. Kaplan, "Food Intake and Blood Cholesterol Levels of Community-Based Adults with Mood Disorders," *Boston Medical Center Psychiatry* 12, no. 10 (2012): 10.

16. Mozhgan Torbai et al., "Effects of Nano and Conventional Zinc Oxide on Anxiety-Like Behavior in Male Rats," *Indian Journal of Pharmacology* 45, no. 5 (2013): 508–12; S. B. Sartori et al., "Magnesium Deficiency Induces Anxiety and HPA Axis Dysregulation: Modulation by Therapeutic Drug Treatment," *Neuropharmacology* 62, no. 1 (2012): 304–12.

17. Joshua J. Broman-Fulks et al., "Effects of Aerobic Exercise on Anxiety Sensitivity," *Behavior Research and Therapy* 42, no. 2 (2004): 125–36.

Chapter 5 How Children Think and What They Think Affect Anxiety

1. David B. Chamberlain, "The Sentient Prenate: What Every Parent Should Know," *Journal of Prenatal and Perinatal Psychology and Health* 26, no. 1 (1996): 37–59.

2. N. J. Smelser and P. B. Baltes, eds., *Encyclopedia of the Social and Behavioral Sciences*, 1st ed. (Oxford: Elsevier Science LTD, 2001), 9683–87.

3. David Howe, "Parent-Reported Problems in 211 Adopted Children: Some Risk and Protective Factors," *Journal of Child Psychology and Psychiatry and Allied Disciplines* 38, no. 4 (1997): 401–11.

4. David G. Meyers and C. Nathan DeWall, *Exploring Psychology*, 10th ed. (New York: Worth, 2016), 285.

5. Meyers and DeWall, *Exploring Psychology*, 285.

6. Daniel L. Schacter, *Searching for Memory: The Brain, the Mind, and the Past* (New York: Basic Books, 1996), 17.

7. Schacter, *Searching for Memory*, 17.

8. Schacter, *Searching for Memory*, 17.

9. Daniel J. Siegel and Tina Payne Bryson, *The Power of Showing Up: How Parental Presence Shapes Who Our Kids Become and How Their Brains Get Wired* (New York: Ballantine, 2020), 31–61.

10. Moïra Milkolajczak, James J. Gross, and Isabelle Roskam, "Parental Burnout: What Is It, and Why Does It Matter?," *Clinical Psychological Science* 7, no. 6 (2019): 1319–29.

11. Marinus H. van Ijzendoorn, Carlo Schuengel, and Marian J. Bakermans-Kranenburg, "Disorganized Attachment in Early Childhood: Meta-analysis of Precursors, Concomitants, and Sequelae," *Development and Psychopathology* 11, no. 2 (1999): 225–49.

12. van Ijzendoorn, Schuengel, and Bakermans-Kranenburg, "Disorganized Attachment in Early Childhood."

13. Meyers and DeWall, *Exploring Psychology*, 143.

Chapter 6 Social Environments Affect Anxiety

1. Denise A. Chavira and Murray B. Stein, "Childhood Social Anxiety Disorder: From Understanding to Treatment," *Child and Adolescent Psychiatric Clinics of North America* 14, no. 4 (October 2005): 797–818.

2. "What Is Stress?," The American Institute of Stress, accessed August 19, 2021, https://www.stress.org/what-is-stress.

3. Meyers and DeWall, *Exploring Psychology*, 368–69.

4. Kenneth R. Ginsburg, the Committee on Communications, and the Committee on Psychosocial Aspects of Child and Family Health, "The Importance of Play in Promoting Healthy Child Development and Maintaining Strong Parent-Child Bonds," *Pediatrics* 119, no. 1 (January 2007): 182–91.

5. G. E. Miller, "The U.S. Is the Most Overworked Developed Nation in the World," *20 Something Finance*, January 13, 2020, https://20somethingfinance .com/american-hours-worked-productivity-vacation.

6. Jean M. Twenge et al., "Birth Cohort Increases in Psychopathology among Young Americans, 1938–2007: A Cross-Temporal Meta-Analysis of the MMPI," *Clinical Psychology Review* 30 (March 2010): 145–54.

7. Joe L. Frost, *A History of Children's Play and Play Environments: Toward a Contemporary Child-Saving Movement* (New York: Routledge, 2010), 199–200, 230–35.

8. Taylor & Francis Group, "Are Your Children Overdoing It? Too Many Extracurricular Activities Can Do More Harm Than Good," *Science Daily*, May 14, 2018, https://www.sciencedaily.com/releases/2018/05/180514122423.htm.

9. "The Impact of Media Use and Screen Time on Children, Adolescents, and Families," American College of Pediatricians, November 2016, https://www .acpeds.org/position-statements/the-impact-of-media-use-and-screen-time-on -children-adolescents-and-families.

10. Twenge et al., "Birth Cohort Increases in Psychopathology among Young Americans," 150.

11. Stanley Rachman, "Betrayal: A Psychological Analysis," *Behavioral Research and Therapy* 48, no. 4 (April 2010): 304–11.

12. Rhea M. Chase and Donna B. Pincus, "Sleep-Related Problems in Children and Adolescents with Anxiety Disorders," *Behavioral Sleep Medicine* 9, no. 4 (2011): 224–36.

13. Ginsburg et al., "The Importance of Play," 182–91.

14. Frank J. Elgar, Wendy Craig, and Stephen J. Trites, "Family Dinners, Communication, and Mental Health in Canadian Adolescents," *Journal of Adolescent Health* 52, no. 4 (2013): 433–38.

15. Douglas A. Gentile et al., "Well-Child Visits in the Video Age: Pediatrics and the American Academy of Pediatrics' Guidelines for Children's Media Use," *Pediatrics* 114, no. 5 (2004): 1235–41.

16. Maria A. Rogers et al., "Parental Involvement and Children's School Achievement: Evidence for Mediating Processes," *Canadian Journal of School Psychology* 24, no. 1 (2009): 34–57.

17. Sharon Wheeler and Ken Green, "The Helping, the Fixtures, the Kits, the Gear, the Gum Shields, the Food, the Snacks, the Waiting, the Rain, the Car Rides . . . : Social Class, Parenting and Children's Organised Activities," *Sport, Education and Society* 24, no. 8 (April 2018): 788–800.

Chapter 7 Children's View of God Affects Anxiety

1. Myers and DeWall, *Exploring Psychology*, 306.

2. William Morris, ed., s.v. "patient," *The American Heritage Dictionary of the English Language* (Boston: Houghton Mifflin Company, 1981), 961.

3. Thesaurus.com, s.v. "patient," accessed August 18, 2021, https://www.thesaurus.com/browse/patient?s=t.

4. Thesaurus.com, s.v. "patient," accessed August 18, 2021, https://www.thesaurus.com/browse/patient?s=t.

Chapter 8 Partnering with Your Child

1. *Encyclopedia Britannica Online*, s.v. "tabula rasa," accessed August 18, 2021, https://www.britannica.com/topic/tabula-rasa.

2. Bianca Acevedo et al., "The Functional Highly Sensitive Brain: A Review of the Brain Circuits Underlying Sensory Processing Sensitivity and Seemingly Related Disorders," *Philosophical Transactions of the Royal Society of London* 373, no. 1744 (April 18, 2018): 20170161.

3. Donna B. Pincus et al., "The Implementation of Modified Parent-Child Interaction Therapy for Youth with Separation Anxiety Disorder," *Cognitive and Behavioral Practice* 15, no. 2 (2008): 118–25.

Chapter 9 Taming the Body's Anxiety

1. Mental Health First Aid Staff, *Mental Health First Aid USA, Adult*, 15th ed. (Washington, DC: National Council for Behavioral Health, 2015), 48.

2. Senthilkumar Ramasamy et al., "Progressive Muscle Relaxation Technique on Anxiety and Depression among Persons Affected by Leprosy," *Journal of Exercise Rehabilitation* 14, no. 3 (2018): 375–81, https://doi.org/10.12965/jer.1836158.079.

Chapter 10 Taming Anxious Belief Systems

1. Carol S. Dweck, *Mindset: The New Psychology of Success* (New York: Ballantine, 2016), 6.

2. Dweck, *Mindset*, 24–29.

3. Dweck, *Mindset*, 6.

4. Thorleif Boman, *Hebrew Thought Compared with Greek* (New York: W.W. Norton, 1970), 133–34.

Chapter 12 Taming Anxious Feelings

1. Jill Bolte Taylor, *My Stroke of Insight* (New York: Penguin Group, 2006), 153.

2. Matthew D. Lieberman et al., "Putting Feelings Into Words," *Psychological Science* 18 (2007): 421–28.

3. Adam R. Aron, Trevor W. Robbins, and Russel A. Poldrack, "Inhibition and the Right Inferior Frontal Cortex," *Trends in Cognitive Science* 8, no. 6 (2004): 170–77.

Chapter 14 Moving Forward

1. Alan Deutschman, *Change or Die: Could You Change When Change Matters Most?* (New York: HarperBusiness, 2005), 53–59, 94.

2. D. O. Hebb, *The Organization of Behavior: A Neuropsychological Theory* (New York: Wiley, 1949).

3. L. P. Spear, "The Adolescent Brain and Age-Related Behavioral Manifestations," *Neuroscience Biobehavioral Review* 24, no. 4 (2000): 417–63.

Appendix A Attachment Style Inventory

1. Adapted from Amir Levine and Rachel Heller, *Attached: The New Science of Adult Attachment and How It Can Help You Find—and Keep—Love* (New York: Penguin Random House, 2010).

About the Author

Jean Holthaus, LISW, LMSW, has practiced as a clinical social worker since 1995. In addition to her clinical work, Jean manages two outpatient clinics and is a regional director for Pine Rest Christian Mental Health Services. She earned a BA in elementary education from the University of Northern Iowa and was an elementary and junior high school teacher for ten years prior to getting her MSW from the University of Iowa. She is passionate about equipping individuals, families, and churches and frequently speaks and presents workshops on a variety of mental health topics. Michelle and Michael are her two adult children, and she enjoys spending time with each of them.

Jean is also the author of *Managing Worry and Anxiety* and currently lives in Grand Rapids, Michigan. For more information, visit www.linkedin.com/in/jeanholthaus.